# I've Heard The Voice of God ~ And I'm No Angel

## Dyan Parker

### A Memoir

Generous Giver Publishing 2015
Nashua, New Hampshire 03063

**Generous Giver Publishing**

ISBN-13: 978-0692585252

ISBN-10: 0692585257

# Dedicated to

My loving parents, Fred and Lorraine, whose unconditional love shaped my inner confidence while not breaking my spirit; my brother, Mike, my best audience and the first to appreciate my humor; my wonderful sisters, Pat and Nan, whose emotional and financial support carried me when I could not walk; my favorite brother-in-law, Peter, the Generous Giver; and of course, God, who has given me the undeserved honor of hearing His Voice, along with the enormous responsibility of sharing His message that *He is real*.

# TABLE OF CONTENTS

I've Heard The
Voice of God ~
And I'm No Angel

# PREFACE

## I've Heard the Voice of God!

People often laugh when I say that I've heard the Voice of God. They think I'm kidding, but I'm not. It sounds irrational to me, too, but it's true. I have actually heard an audible masculine voice speak to me and it has happened more than once. It always took me by surprise; a few times I was praying, searching for an answer, but never expecting a reply.

I had always assumed there were many who had also heard His Voice. After extensive research I realize that my experience is extraordinary.

Not only have I heard the Voice of God, one night I actually had a conversation with Him. I just had a painful revelation and was crying in my car, talking out loud to God. That's when He spoke to me. Startled and stunned at first, I sobbed back my response. He replied again, which immediately brought peace to my troubled heart.

At the time the wonderment of having a conversation with God did not register. What mattered more was what He said to me. It was the only time there was a dialogue instead of my just hearing Him. As I replay that evening in my mind, it never fails to amaze me. It sounds unbelievable and I'm still in total awe. Why did this happen and how could I have been so blessed to have it happen to me? To be sure, it's an undeserved honor.

My life continues to be a tapestry of unexplainable events. Nonbelievers would call them coincidences. I say they are instances where God remains anonymous. I call them *God-winks*.

**Heaven Is For Real**

What made me write this book? I read the first page of *Heaven Is For Real: A Little Boy's Astounding Story of His Trip to Heaven and Back* by Todd Burpo. "If you're ready to go to heaven this book will inspire you, if you're not, let this child lead you." My first thought was some people don't think about Heaven because they don't believe in God. It was immediately followed by a strong suggestion to write about *my* experiences. I needed to tell the nonbelievers that God is real. It all happened in a nanosecond. The idea was born but I did nothing about it.

**The Daily Word Booklet**

My wonderful grandmother was almost 100 when she had a piercing gallbladder attack. We wanted her to make it to her centennial birthday bash but her health was our main concern. When the doctor told Gram that she needed immediate surgery, she said, "Okay, let's do it." Then he changed his mind and whispered to us that she was too frail. Gram replied, "Then I just want to go home." What he didn't tell her, but told the family, was that she had only a few weeks to live. Her gallbladder was infected and the infection would go through her entire seventy-six pound body. We were devastated by the news.

I requested prayers from everyone who crossed my path. Several churches added her name to their special intentions and prayer lists. During this time The Unity Church's *Daily Word* magazine started to arrive in my mailbox once a month but I didn't read any of them, nor did I throw them away. They piled up on my bedroom floor.

When the tenth envelope came from Unity I unwrapped the booklet and put it on the kitchen counter. It opened to a page and my eyes fell to the first words: "If I told you that God actually spoke to me, you might think I'm nuts." I was overjoyed. I had been searching everywhere to find *someone* who had also heard the Voice of God. Now this little booklet opened up to that precise page...what a *God-wink*!

I called my mother later that night and read that story to her. I glanced down, and in the pile next to my bed was another booklet with the same cover. Were my eyes playing tricks on me? Did I already have a copy of this edition? I bent down and picked it up...sure enough, same edition. I would never have found the time to read any of those booklets. God wanted me to know that He recently had spoken to someone else and to encourage me to start writing.

## A Quick Overview

People say I'm a hard worker, and a fun, sociable, and energetic person. I don't drink alcohol nor do I use drugs. I'm not on any medication and have no history of mental illness. My family is average, middle-class. My parents were married for more than sixty-five years. I have an older brother, two younger sisters, and two generations of nieces and nephews. My grandmother is 103. I am a law-abiding citizen and I have great respect for everyone, especially seniors and our military.

This is just a quick snapshot of me. What you are about to read happened to an ordinary person. You may think this is fiction when, in fact, it is the truth...every last word. This is exactly what happened.

**God Is Real**

Here is my account of not only the times that I've heard the Voice of God but several *God-winks*. I don't have to look far to know that God is in my daily happenings; some are more profound than others. Many are funny; God has an amazing sense of humor. If you believe in God, you'll enjoy my memoir. If you don't, then maybe this book will help you be open to believing that God is real. I know He is because He spoke to me; I've heard Him. I've heard the Voice of God ~ and I'm no Angel.

*"This is what the Lord, the God of Israel, says: 'Write in a book all the words I have spoken to you.' "* ~ Jeremiah 30:2

# CHAPTER 1 ~ THE FIRST TIME

*"Jesus said, 'Whoever belongs to God hears what God says.'"* ~ John 8:47

## If You Abuse These

I was a cocktail waitress at a ritzy jazz club on Cape Cod and the nightlife was captivating. Working past midnight and then partying 'til dawn thrilled me. As a recent graduate at 22, it was the first time I was on my own: no parents, no teachers, no rules, and no limits. My newfound freedom was worlds away from the all-girls' Catholic college that I attended the previous four years.

The taste of alcohol and its effects never appealed to me. Diet pills held my interest. I constantly battled with the same five-to-ten stubborn pounds. My head was definitely fatter than my hips. I was elated when a friend introduced me to a doctor who guaranteed his little blue pills would melt away my fat. The capsules were amazing. They helped me stay busy, they provided tons of energy and were perfect for partying all night. I never wanted to eat and they made me thin. What's not to like?

On the third visit to that doctor, he immediately wrote me out a prescription. He put me on the scale to check my weight and then proceeded to write out another script. When I realized what he was doing I got excited, too excited. I didn't want him to remember he had already written the prescription. I started to manipulate the conversation, deliberately trying to distract him. It worked.

While walking to my car I felt victorious and cheered to myself, "Yes! Two prescriptions! Yes!" Then a masculine voice calmly said, *"If you abuse these you will be in big trouble."* It stopped me in my tracks. I looked around. There was no one else in the parking lot. I couldn't tell where the sound came from but the warning was true. I *did* fully intend to abuse them. I ripped up those two pieces of paper before I got to my car.

I sat in my car, still shaking from the experience. I realized that I liked those pills way too much to use them as prescribed. They definitely were getting addictive. The gentle caution was a much-needed reality slap that forced me to face my true intentions. Although this was the first time I heard that Voice it would not be the last.

**The Last Convertible**

My dad bought me an adorable *LeMans* convertible when I was a senior in college. I loved it. Nothing made me happier than driving and getting tan at the same time, while the wind blew through my hair. On the first gorgeous Cape Cod day the following spring I couldn't wait to remove the restraints of the roof. Although it was still a tad too cold to be cruising, it was perfect weather when parked. A friend and I drove to the beach and found a nice spot facing the ocean. I put the top down and we devoured a delicious lunch while the sun showered us with warm kisses. When it was time to leave I pushed the button to secure the canvas and drove back to her workplace. As she shut the door while saying good-bye, the entire passenger window shattered. Little pebble-like pieces of glass were everywhere! We were in shock. The roof and the window had not lined up. My first thought was, "How am I going to pay for this?" There was plenty of time to worry. I would be driving for the next hour to attend an engagement party my parents were hosting for my sister, Patty.

As I drove, my brain was spinning with panic. I was fearful that the glass would not be covered by my limited insurance. I had visions of not being able to use my car until I had the funds to repair the gaping hole. What would happen if it rained in the meantime? An uninvited idea danced into my thoughts. I could give the insurance company a plausible scenario that *would* be covered. My mind went back and forth with different lies. The one that seemed the most believable was theft. "Someone broke into my car and stole valuable things." Versions of this deceitful notion kept me preoccupied for the next thirty minutes.

I approached a roadside flower stand. I always stopped there when going to my parents. I planned to stop there again. Route 44's four-lane highway was busy and I needed to take a left-turn. With my blinker on, I waited for the oncoming traffic to subside. Then someone rear-ended my car so hard that it knocked me out.

When I opened my eyes, I was dazed and confused. "Why did someone just hit me over the head with a sledgehammer?" The sound of a screaming baby brought me back to reality. I got out of my smashed car and staggered toward the vehicle that was now crushed and attached to the back of mine. The sixteen-year-old driver was too drunk to get out of her wreck. I held and comforted her crying infant until the ambulance took us to the hospital. The impact was so severe that both cars were totaled; it was a miracle we were not injured.

Later that night there was a segment on TV, "The Last Convertible," announcing it was the last day convertibles would be made. It would be years before automakers would manufacture convertible sedans again. How fitting that I would total mine on the day that the last ragtop rolled out on the assembly line. I would have to wait a long time before getting my next one.

My coverage did not include collision. The teenager who hit me did not have any insurance. I was devastated. My favorite car didn't just have a broken window, it was demolished. What haunted me more was my devious solution earlier that day. I had been so willing to compromise my values and make a fraudulent insurance claim. An hour later that was not even an option; my entire vehicle was smashed. It was a costly lesson. My convertible was destroyed but my integrity was protected, through no means of my own.

## Rick

I met Rick when I was 25. He was a local Cape Cod police officer and I had just opened a dance studio. My sister, Nancy, had a blind date with him and they were meeting at midnight after their second shift jobs. Since she had recently moved to the Cape and didn't know the area, I offered to go with her. Unbeknown to me, Rick was the same policeman who had stopped me months before for a traffic violation. When he called me the next day instead of calling my sister, I was a little unsure about accepting. Nan quickly gave me her blessing.

Rick was a good man: reliable, trustworthy and different than most of the men I had dated. For one thing, he was not a big drinker. The highs and lows of the alcoholic personality were attractive to me. It was somewhat like a roller coaster, never knowing what to expect. Rick was a tad predictable. He was also built like Buddha, the typical cop who loved donuts. At least he would always be bigger

5

than me. Many of my past boyfriends were slim and I always had the fear of being the fat wife with the frail husband. The biggest difference was that I didn't lust after Rick. In my naïve little mind I thought if it wasn't lust it must be love. With those three strong redeeming qualities he soon became perfect husband material. Within nine months we married.

Three months later I could not stop the batches of holiday gingerbread men from jumping into my mouth. I gained ten pounds. Desperate and afraid, I searched for something to help me lose weight and it could not be diet pills. That's when I found My Anonymous Program. At my first MAP meeting they introduced a new term, compulsive eating. They said that overeating would be my most natural reaction to life. Happy, sad, mad, or glad, it didn't matter, eating was always on my mind, and needless to say it was never broccoli. I found it easier to stuff my face than to face my stuff. I had a physical addiction with a mental obsession and they said that the solution was spiritual. I started to attend on a regular basis. It helped.

My world was soon shattered with the news that Rick was chosen to be a K-9 Customs Agent. We would be moving to Virginia. He was elated and I was crushed. My family and friends meant the world to me but he didn't have any close connections to tie him to the Cape. He was not close to anyone. He had once casually mentioned that when he was eleven, his mother was in the hospital. One day he walked into her room and found her bed empty. What a horrible way to find out his mother had died that morning. It was the one and only time he talked about his mom. His heart broke that day. He shut down his emotions and unconsciously vowed never to care about anyone ever again. It would take years for me to realize that I was not an exception.

**The Greatest Miracle**

Somewhere along the way *The Greatest Miracle in the World* by Og Mandino fell into my hands. It contained "The God Memorandum". I was supposed to read it for one hundred consecutive nights. The book also suggested pinning a half-inch square of white cloth on my clothes, as a rag picker's secret amulet. I was changing my life from the pins and rags of failure to the treasures of a new and better life. I performed this ritual nightly. There were many times when I fell into bed exhausted, almost too tired to see. I faithfully completed the exercise for the hundred days.

The Memorandum started with a comforting idea:

> To You, From God:
> *Feel my hand. Hear my words.*
> *You need me ... and I need you.*
> *We have a world to rebuild.*
> *And if it requires a miracle what is that to us?*
> *We are both miracles and now we have each other.*

Although I had always believed in God, I thought that I would only see Him when I died. There was never a belief that I could have a conscious contact with Him on a daily basis. When I finished the hundred days of "The God Memorandum" my relationship with Him began.

## CHAPTER 2 ~ THE SECOND TIME

*"Jesus answered, 'My sheep listen to my voice; I know them, and they follow me.' "* ~ John 10:27

### You Will Sell Your Car

We had been living in Virginia Beach for less than a year. It was time to move back to New England for another promotion. Rick had bought me a TR-6 sports car convertible when we first arrived. It was a perfect vehicle to have in Virginia but it was not practical for Cape Cod. Going back to Massachusetts in the fall would not be the best place for my adorable little beauty. I was so torn because I loved my car and did not want to give it up.

Rick had already moved and I was to follow him once he finished his three-month orientation. During this transition time my car radiator sprang a leak. My prayer was, "God, if You help me fix this with ninety-nine-cent gunk, I will sell my car." The magic potion from 7-Eleven instantly stopped the dripping. I immediately made a sign that said "BUY ME."

We lived off a major highway and every day after work I strategically parked my car on the busy street corner, placed the sign on the windshield, and walked a short distance to my home.

For weeks I packed dishes, pictures, and other household items. One day as I went into my dining room, the table was bare except for two brads. You know, the little nails used to hang pictures. They were in the sign of a cross. I didn't put them there. When I saw them I immediately heard, *"You will sell your car by 7:30."* It was the same masculine voice I had heard years before. It startled me but I wasn't afraid; it was just weird. It took me totally by surprise. It was dinnertime and I had only been thinking about eating, not about selling my car.

My evening activities continued without interruption. I resisted the urge to look at the clock. I was upstairs in the bedroom when the telephone rang. I picked it up and with excitement in my voice said, "Hello?" The caller asked, "Did you sell your car yet?" When I answered, "No," he replied, "Great. I'm going to buy it and I have the cash." That was that. I looked at the clock and it was 7:27...I sold my car by 7:30!

**I Want To Be Baptized Again**

We weren't back on the Cape for long when Rick decided he wanted to move to Georgia. He would be an instructor at the Federal Law Enforcement Training Center. It was a big promotion for him but I didn't want to go. My MAP group was super, my neighbors were great and I loved being back in New England near my family. The more comfortable I felt, the less settled Rick was.

He went ahead of me, again, in search of the perfect job. I followed him three months later.

While in Georgia I attended a Bible study class. I read that Jesus told his Apostles to teach all nations and baptize them. My parents had me christened at three weeks old. No one "taught" me as an infant. That Bible class got me thinking about getting baptized again. It surprised me at how insistent I felt about this while talking to the priest later that week. He was not cooperative at all. He said, "No. We believe in one baptism for the forgiveness of sins. You are already baptized." To me, it was a matter of principle.

Rick and I went to the Catholic Church every Saturday night, and I taught Sunday school the next morning. Since this happened around Thanksgiving there was no religious instruction that weekend. I decided to visit the local Baptist Church that Sunday. I had never been there before but felt a strong desire to go, and went alone. At the end of the service they made an announcement. "By the way, we're having Baptism this afternoon. If anyone would like to be baptized, come on back." I was delighted. At two o'clock I returned to the church, put on a white robe and walked into a pool of water. Gratitude filled my heart. God orchestrated several unconnected incidents for that day to happen. I was thrilled to be baptized again.

## Turning 33

We stayed in Georgia for four years. Then Rick received a huge promotion, which meant another move. This time it was to Boston and we were beyond excited to be moving back north. I just turned 33. Digital clocks just started to be popular and 33s were everywhere. It took me a while to make the connection that Christ was 33 when He died, so to me 33 was a holy number. Not that I thought much about it but 666 is the sign of the devil and is the exact opposite of 33. My theory is that Satan knew 33 represented Jesus. Satan tried to be superior so he picked 66 for his number, only to rethink it and decided that 666 would be even better. Ever since then, 33 has always been an important number for me. When I was being obedient, doing the right thing, the time would be 7:33 or 11:33...3:33 was always the best. If I had just yelled at somebody, eaten some junk food, or was fearful about something, the clock would be 6:34 or 9:34. I've also been saying "I'm 33 again" for many years. As I type this it's 10:33 on the clock.

## CHAPTER 3 ~ THE THIRD TIME

*"Jesus said to His Disciples, 'For I tell you that many prophets and kings wanted to see what you see but did not see it, and to hear what you hear but did not hear it.' "*
~ Luke 10:24

### No Amount of Food

Since junk food had been my favorite source of nourishment for many years prior to MAP, it was not surprising that I had my share of dental problems. We had just moved back to New England when I had another toothache. The new dentist suggested a specialist who told me that surgery was necessary. There was a good chance the right side of my face would be partially paralyzed due to the condition of a back tooth. I flipped out. I possess a touch of vanity and having half of my face paralyzed was something impossible for me to accept.

After I scheduled the surgery, my first panicked thought while walking to my car was, "Oh my God, what can I eat?" I wasn't talking to God; it was just an expression. You can imagine my surprise when His Voice answered back, *"No amount of food will fix your tooth."*

I never made the connection that overeating wouldn't fix anything. Nor did I realize that it always made things worse. The problem would still exist and there would also be the extra weight. That day was different. Although I had been going to MAP for eight years, it was the first time I connected the dots. Junk food would not help my tooth or *any* situation. So, I asked God to help me to not think of overeating, even though all I wanted to do was bury my feelings and fears in food. Again, I needed to face my stuff, not stuff my face. I had to forget about my tooth and take one day at a time. I needed to keep it in the NOW, and not panic about my face potentially being paralyzed. I only needed to deal with that on the day of the surgery, which was three weeks away.

This happened during the Christmas season. Rick and I were having a New Year's Eve party and I made sure that all the food at our party was free of sugar, flour, and alcohol. No one seemed to notice there was no junk food. Everyone said it was the best celebration - we concentrated on the company, not the snacks. All we did was laugh, play games, and make silly party hats. The bonus was I didn't wake up the first day of the New Year determined to start yet another diet. My operation was scheduled for the following week.

On the day of the surgery, as standard procedure, they took another x-ray. They wanted to see how much the tooth had declined. After looking at the image the doctor shook his head and announced, "This is so strange! Your tooth is fine; there's nothing wrong with it. We don't need to operate."

I knew that God fixed my tooth because I was obedient. It's easy to be compliant when that's what I want to do but every part of me screamed to dull the pain by escaping into food. It wasn't physical pain but rather the fear-pain – panic of the consequences of that surgery, and dread of having half my face paralyzed.

*"No amount of food will fix your tooth."* Hearing the Voice of God made me realize that overeating was not an option. It was so hard, yet so worth the price of not giving into the fear...or the food. I skipped out of the surgeon's office that day. I was not only joyous but several pounds lighter than when I walked in three weeks earlier.

## CHAPTER 4 ~ A CONVERSATION WITH GOD

*"This is what the Lord says, 'Call to me and I will answer you.' "* ~ Jeremiah 33:3

### Admit the Truth

During the nine years of marriage we had moved eleven times. Rick was on the professional fast track, going from one government agency to another. From where I stood, he was definitely more interested in advancing his career than in being a husband. His childhood vow of not getting close to anyone was still alive. He recommitted to it with every promotion. I was more alone than I had ever been.

I was content with my church, family, friends, condo, plants, and work, but not with my marriage. We didn't have much of a marriage. Rick, then a Drug Enforcement Agent, was gone most of the time. My mantra was, "I'm a single married person. I can do whatever I want, except have a date on Saturday night."

My dad told me of a business called Undercover Wear, a designer lingerie company that promoted home parties for women. I immediately joined the company. While doing a show on Cape Cod a strong emotion overcame me. I was in a lovely home with a darling wife, doting husband and their adorable baby. I was happy for them but so sad for myself. At that moment it became clear to me that having a loving family life would not be my path with Rick.

The women bought more lingerie if they had sugar in their systems so I always brought chocolate to my shows. Normal people can eat candy. I cannot. It's a poison for me and it sets up an insatiable craving. While driving home that night on the deserted highway my hand fished for the sweets in the back seat. After several handfuls I started to cry. "God, I have been in MAP for nine years and I'm still eating candy. What's wrong?" In the stillness of the night I heard, *"Admit the truth and the truth will set you free."* My heart raced and I could feel the shakiness in my limbs. Hearing His Voice surprised, startled and somewhat scared me. The darkness didn't help. I didn't want to admit what I was trying to stuff. I answered Him back, sobbing through my words, "The truth is I don't want to be married to Rick anymore." God calmly replied, *"Then tell him."*

The memory of this still takes my breath away. I had a conversation with God! We not only had a dialogue but He gave me permission to not be married anymore. I was a good Catholic girl, having gone to parochial schools for seventeen years. In my mind marriage was forever. I had not consciously been thinking of divorce. I would have thought that God would have said, "Try harder." Or "Go to counseling." Or "Don't give up." Or "Do a Marriage Encounter." But He didn't. He simply said, *"Then tell him."* It was the same calm masculine Voice that I heard before.

My home was an hour away and my mind raced. Questions started to whirl in my brain. Where to go? How to live? What about money? Solutions started to accompany them just as fast. My friend Paula had an extra room. My parents would love to have me stay with them. It didn't matter where I went as long as I left.

I started talking out loud to God again. "Okay, God, if You really want me to tell him, have him be home." Since Rick was a DEA Agent, there were many times I would get in late and Rick would not be there yet. So tonight he needed to be home. Getting closer to home, I said again, "All right, God, if You really want me to tell him, have him be awake." Often I would get home and Rick would be sleeping – he needed to be awake tonight. Getting closer, I continued, "God, if You really want me to tell him, have him be up." I didn't want to talk to Rick if he were in bed. Driving into my condo complex I said, "Please God, if You really want me to tell him, please give me the strength."

As I drove around the corner I was surprised to see that Rick was just getting out of his car. I took a deep breath and said another quick prayer for courage. I parked my car next to his and said as I got out, "I'm so glad you're here, I have something I want to talk to you about." "How much is it going to cost me?" was his sarcastic reply. "Nothing," was my answer. "You wrecked the car?" was his second response. "No, I didn't wreck the car." His third guess was, "You want a divorce?" I could not believe my ears. All I could say was, "Bingo!"

What a miracle. It had only been an hour since my conversation with God and now it was Rick who said the word DIVORCE, not me. Once we got into the house I said, "I don't love you the way a wife should love a husband. You deserve the prettiest girl on Cape Cod and three kids, but it's not me. I don't want to disrupt your house. I'm not going to take anything. I just want to come back and water my plants." I felt enormous relief at that moment, so free, so happy and so honest. I had finally admitted the truth, a truth that I wasn't even consciously aware of, and I was set free.

## Life Is Too Short

The next day I woke up relieved and filled with hope. I couldn't wait to get outside and go for a bicycle ride. I didn't want to stop pedaling my bike on that glorious, warm spring afternoon. My mind kept replaying the night before and my conversation with God and everything else that followed. Cycling past a cemetery on my left, I heard the Voice of God again. This time He said, *"Life is too short to be miserable; be honest with yourself and be honest with others."* I smiled in agreement at the simple advice and was grateful to have had the courage to be honest. While biking through unfamiliar neighborhoods I ended up going by the same cemetery. I heard The Voice, just a little bit louder the second time. *"Life is too short to be miserable; be honest with yourself and be honest with others."*

Three days later Rick called. He had been transferred again and he wanted to start over, so I could keep everything. Awesome! I believe that God gave me everything because I was willing to take nothing. My freedom was all I wanted. God was instrumental in this breakup so it was no surprise at how it all was unfolding. Things were moving fast and I felt in sync with The King of the Universe.

## Perfect Timing

Rick and I had bought a brand-new townhouse the previous year at pre-construction pricing. I couldn't afford to stay there by myself so we agreed to sell it and split the profits. My ad in the local newspaper immediately attracted an engaged couple. They wanted to close on the condo in three months, which was perfect timing for me. We made $50,000, which was unheard of at the time. God was making this a smooth transition and I was extremely grateful.

## Santo Domingo

After telling Rick how I felt, my thoughts immediately focused on getting a divorce. Since we didn't own anything other than the townhouse, we would be able to do it without a lawyer. After a little investigating I realized an uncontested divorce would cost very little. It would take six months to petition the courts. That was too long for me to wait. I wanted out NOW. My travel agent suggested a twenty-four-hour divorce. My choices were Reno, Nevada, or Santo Domingo, Dominican Republic. Santo Domingo sounded more exotic. I was excited about getting divorced and taking a vacation at the same time.

A week before the trip, my friend Linda asked if she could go with me. What great news! Although I was willing to go alone, it wasn't my first choice. Walking so closely with God made me feel invincible and protected, but a female traveling alone would not have been smart. We boarded the plane and headed to Santo Domingo without having any idea of what we were getting into.

When we landed, a sea of men jammed the airport – not a female in sight. My nervous plea to Linda was, "Let's not talk to anyone unless they are wearing a cross." That didn't help; everyone had a crucifix around their neck and some were as large as dinner plates.

We were relieved to have a bus driver approach us saying, "Americana? Americana?" We nodded and followed him to a waiting bus. Our calmness quickly turned to panic. He was not asking us if we were Americans, he was going to the Americana Hotel. We learned almost too late that he was driving in the opposite direction of where we needed to go. We hopped off the bus just before it left the airport. By that time, everyone was gone from the area; there was not a soul to be seen. No buses, no cars, no people. The area was deserted. We were alone, stunned, and totally vulnerable.

An old jalopy soon came by, tooting the horn, yelling to us, "Taxi. Taxi." About the same time, a police officer came out of the airport. We questioned whether the rattletrap was a taxi and he replied, "Sí, taxi." Linda and I hesitantly climbed in the back seat of the beat up car. We prayed out loud during the entire forty-minute ride to the center of Santo Domingo. He dropped us off at our hotel, as promised, and we were relieved that we had not been abducted.

The next day was the court date with my Spanglish-speaking lawyer. When it was our turn to enter the judge's chambers I said a quick little prayer and walked in with my stack of documents. The magistrate examined and checked off everything. When he got to the bottom of the pile he took off his glasses. He gave me a confused look and questioned the whereabouts of my marriage certificate. My church license was in the pile of papers but my state certificate that had arrived in the mail the week before was still on my desk in Massachusetts. I wanted to vomit.

The judge just smiled at me. With a slight British accent, he said, "It is like going hunting and forgetting the bullets. You did not come all this way for a divorce if you are not married. Divorced!" Drawing the biggest sigh of relief, I wanted to give him a hug but all I could muster was, "Thank you. Thank you. Thank you," in a choked-up voice with tears ready to spill. Only God could have given me a gracious judge with a sense of humor and a logical mind.

## The Annulment

Returning home from Santo Domingo as a divorced woman was a great relief but there was one more step to take. I walked across the street to the rectory, the place where priests live. I inquired about getting an annulment. Since this was not a real marriage in my mind, I felt it shouldn't be on my record. To me, it didn't matter that we were married for nine years; it was a nine-year farce. We were never a couple and it should be erased.

The annulment process was quite lengthy. I needed three witnesses plus myself to answer seventy-five questions. Twenty-five questions were about us as a couple. Twenty-five were about me and then twenty-five more about Rick. My mom, sister, and friend Nancy F. agreed to be witnesses. It didn't take long for us to complete the documents and I submitted them eagerly. After two months of waiting, the Diocesan of Fall River received a call from me to check on the status. They claimed they didn't have any paperwork on my annulment. I was horrified. What happened to it? I immediately called the priest and he casually said to me, "Oh, it hasn't been submitted yet. I'm still waiting for you to give me your marriage certificate from the state." I was furious. "When were you going to tell me that you were missing something?" He didn't have an answer for me. Priest or no priest, this man dropped the ball. There were no apologies, just excuses from him. At that moment my respect for him evaporated. Within minutes I stormed over to the rectory with a copy of the lost document. I was so angry I could not even look at him. Having resentment is like drinking poison expecting the other person to die. That priest was at the top of my resentment list. I even stopped going to that church. Whom was I really hurting?

Two years later the notification arrived stating that the marriage was annulled. During their investigation it was necessary to seek the opinion of a psychological expert. The fee was $180. Getting an annulment for under $200 was unheard of. Most people pay several hundred, if not thousands, of dollars. This was just another reason to say, "Thank You, God."

# CHAPTER 5 ~ MY DATING COACH

*"Jesus said, 'What I tell you in the dark, speak in the daylight; what is whispered in your ear, proclaim from the roofs.' "* ~ Matthew 10: 27

## Go With Someone for Who They Are

As a newly divorced woman I was eager to get back in the dating scene. When my ex-husband left the house and moved back to the Cape, I immediately started to socialize. I was starved for attention. I met MD at my first dance. He was cute, charming, and a great dancer. The attraction was mutual. He was also a recovering alcoholic-drug addict. Louie, the consultant at work, also held my interest. Not knowing much about Lou other than he was available and had lots of money, he was on my list to check out. I liked both MD and Louie but for different reasons. Since I just had that wonderful experience with God giving me permission to divorce, I kiddingly asked His thoughts about which guy I should date. His answer spoke to my spirit and said, *"Go with someone for who they are, not for what they have."* WOW. That made it clear! The man from the dance won my heart.

## It's Okay

The elation of being divorced was exhilarating. When I started dating MD, he replaced much of the time that I had spent praising, praying and thanking God. MD was also spiritual, so we talked a lot about God and all the wonderful things that He had done for us. It hadn't even occurred to me that I was giving God less attention.

One night, driving on the highway that exact thought occurred to me. I spoke out loud. "I'm sorry, God, for not spending as much time with You, but I'm so happy to be with MD. He takes up time that used to be spent with You. I'm really enjoying him and he's such a great man." At that moment, a car came from my right side, swerved in front of me and the license plate was *ITS OK*. I just laughed and said, "God, You are so funny." Of course I'm not supposed to be a saint, or to be just thinking about God and praying 24/7. I live in the real world, interacting with people. It's natural wanting to love someone and have someone love me back. I was really feeling bad that God might have missed my company. It was comforting to get the reassurance that it was okay.

## Rent Out Your Rooms

Two years passed since MD and I met at that dance. We were engaged and had recently bought a house. Unfortunately, we were also arguing a lot and it was evident to me that a breakup was imminent. He had been drug free for several years before I met him but he was back on them and life was a nightmare. MD was a military brat and moved around his entire childhood. Because he was somewhat small in stature he was constantly picked on as being the puny new kid. At an early age he found that alcohol eased his pain. When the booze couldn't drown his sorrows he switched to drugs. He soon escalated from marijuana to hard-core opiates. My family was horrified as they watched me leave a respected DEA Agent for a heroin addict.

I needed to get rid of this guy but was not quite sure how. I started to pray and ask for help and guidance. While in my sewing room, the smallest of our four bedrooms, I felt God whisper, *"You could rent out your rooms."* What a great idea. The small room could be mine and I could rent my other three furnished bedrooms. Until then I had no idea what I was going to do financially. The large home was too big and too expensive to live there by myself. Since it was all my down payment, I was definitely going to stay in the house.

When MD moved out, which wasn't without a fight, I put an ad in the local newspaper and immediately found three girls to rent my rooms. We called it a Sober House because alcohol and drugs were not allowed. The girls paid more than enough to cover the mortgage and the utilities. This was a perfect arrangement until the following year when I became an absentee landlord.

## Buy a Bottle of British Sterling

One day at work, I looked out the window and there was MD just sitting in his truck, watching me. My heart jumped; I hadn't seen him in months. I had a civil restraining order on him. He knew how to push my buttons. He was an active drug addict and I became a crazy person when we were together. It had become a toxic relationship and a dangerous combination. Seeing him out in the parking lot gave me instant amnesia and I walked out to see what he wanted. We spoke briefly. Knowing he shouldn't be within one hundred yards of me, I told him not to come back. While I walked away, the lingering scent of his aftershave brought back happy memories. Part of me sighed, "I miss him, I miss the good times...I miss his smell." God interrupted my crazy thoughts. He replaced them with, *"Buy a bottle of British Sterling. It will be cheaper."* I laughed and agreed. MD was nothing but trouble, chaos, and bad news. Yes, buying a bottle of British Sterling would be cheaper.

## You're A Long Way From Home

It was St. Patrick's Day and I was going to a nightclub with Marianne, a casual acquaintance. Because I didn't drink we took my car. When the club closed we went over to a bartender's house to continue partying. After a few hours of mindless chatter with strangers, it was time for me to call it a night. We were still about forty-five minutes from our hometown and I was more than ready to leave. Marianne was preoccupied with one of the guys. Every fifteen minutes I would say, "Marianne, let's go." She would reply, "In a minute," but made no attempt to leave. After repeating that exchange several times I finally said, "I am leaving in five minutes, with or without you." I would have never left my sister or a good friend, I would have dragged them out. Five minutes later she got her last warning. She did not move, so I walked out. One of the guys followed me and asked for a ride back to his car. I welcomed the company because I had no idea where we were.

We got into my car and as he told me where to turn I started to notice how eerie he looked. Although we had been chatting a little back at the house I didn't know anything about this guy. Other than telling me which way to go, he hadn't said anything. Then he uttered in a creepy voice, "Would you like to make love tonight?" I instantly got a sick feeling but tried to use a happy tone when I replied, "No, thank you." The silence in the car was awkward but I thought the subject had been forgotten. Three long minutes later the only thing he said was, "Why not?" The hair on the back of my neck stood up – I was now afraid. All the articles in women's magazines about this kind of situation flashed through my brain. Fear raced through my body and my nervous words were, "Oh, we really don't know each other well. We don't know each other at all, but thanks anyway." I was trying to sound cheerful and not as terrified as I felt. He replied a moment later, in a sinister voice, "You're a long way from home and you don't have a clue where you are." I knew then that I was in trouble, big trouble, and I was scared to death.

I was frantically praying as my mind started spinning. The next words that came out of my mouth were, "Well, if we were to do that we would go to a hotel, wouldn't we? There are many hotels on Route 1." My real intention was to get to that populated area and find some help. He seemed to be appeased. We were then able to make some small talk. It was idle babble while I was panicking, praying, and looking for a way to escape.

We finally came to the Route 1 intersection. Across the street I saw the Massachusetts State Police Barracks. Relief overcame me and I wanted to cry. My car crossed the four-lane highway and sped into that parking lot. I jumped out of the car even faster, ran up the stairs as if he were chasing me, and swung opened the heavy glass door. Crying, shaking and talking so fast that my words blurred all together. "There's a man in my car – I don't know him – I was taking him back to his car – He's talking about making love – I don't know him – I'm really scared – I don't want him in my car." Seeing my fright, the trooper didn't hesitate. He went to the door and called to the creep. "Buddy, she doesn't want you in her car. Get out and call a friend." The louse was furious as he removed himself from my vehicle. He was finally out of my car and I knew my exact location. Only then was I able to breathe, although my body was trembling.

After profusely thanking the trooper, I got in my car and drove away. I was not surprised that I was still shaking. It was a dangerous lesson for me to learn about not having strangers in my car. He could have had a gun, a knife, or worse. Thank God he didn't use physical force – he certainly could have. When he was telling me to take the rights and lefts and how to get out of the woods, I was totally at his mercy. I was keeping my cool on the surface but praying like crazy. God heard my prayers, answered them, and sent me the highest law officer in the state to protect me. Thank You, God. I have learned my lesson.

**John Thought It Was Odd**

One of the guys in MAP caught my attention. He was somewhat cute, had a good job, liked going to church, and had older kids. We started dating. Although we had fun, he wasn't the love of my life. After seeing him for several months we both decided that it wasn't a good fit so we stopped dating. John had one major complaint about me. He thought it was odd that every time I would see "33" I would say, "Thirty-three, Thank You, God."

Realizing that initially it would be a bit awkward to see each other at MAP, we agreed to go to different meetings. Since there were many to choose from, it was relatively easy to determine which meetings would be mine and which would be his. The Saturday evening group was the only one up for grabs because neither of us went there on a regular basis.

One Saturday night I really needed a meeting. John's car was in the parking lot as I drove up. Instead of turning around I went inside, walked over to John, and asked if we could talk for a second in the other room. My words were, "I need a meeting and evidently you do, too. I'll flip you for it." He took a quarter out of his pocket, flipped it in the air, called tails and slapped it on his wrist near his watch. He lifted his hand and next to the heads-up quarter his watch read 7:33. I immediately said, "Heads. I win, and oh, it's 7:33–Thank You, God." With that I turned around and confidently walked into the meeting. John followed, grabbed his coat and left; he didn't know what just hit him. Wasn't God cute in making the time 7:33? It still makes me laugh remembering the look on John's face. I bet he pays attention to 33s now.

## CHAPTER 6 ~ CROSSING THE LINE

*"With eyes full of adultery, they never stop sinning; they seduce the unstable; they are experts in greed, an accursed brood!"* ~ 2 Peter 2:14

**Jude**

Sandra asked me to join her at The Villa Restaurant after a Chamber of Commerce event. She was going by herself. I offered to go with her so she wouldn't be alone. These were the same words I said to my sister the night I met Rick. History repeats itself.

While at the restaurant five men walked in. One was tall, blond, and good-looking. I noticed him right away; he was hard to miss. They went into the dining room while we were sitting in the lounge. It was September 24, a date that would prove to be significant in the future. The guys eventually made it over to our area. The cute one was Jude and his friend Phil introduced him as the most eligible man in New Hampshire. I was very attracted to Jude; he was not only nice-looking, he was charming, and he seemed to like me, too. Before I knew it, we had a date for the next evening.

He picked me up in his brand-new limited edition Corvette, which impressed me. We had a wonderful evening. Although he lived four hours north, he was planning to stay the next day. We had another date the following night. He asked me if I wanted to go to New Hampshire the upcoming weekend; it was foliage season and he thought I would enjoy it. My reply was, "Sure, but I'm not going to sleep with you." He assured me that that was not his intention and he would certainly get two hotel rooms. I told him it wouldn't be necessary but I would be sleeping in my pajamas.

The next weekend I drove north to meet Jude halfway. I had a fabulous time riding around the stunning mountains, chatting, and getting to know him. The sleeping accommodations were no problem; he was a gentleman and my pajamas stayed on. We went away for three more weekends until he said one Saturday, "I have something I need to tell you." He seemed a tad somber but he was also a joker, so I wasn't taking him too seriously. I did keep mentioning that my favorite movie was *Fatal Attraction* which seemed to lighten the mood.

When we got back to the hotel room, he sat me down, held my hands, looked straight in my eyes and said, "I'm married." My reaction conveyed my thought that he was kidding. His reply was, "I'm not kidding. I'm married." It felt as if he kicked me in the stomach. I couldn't breathe. Trying hard to hold back my tears, I got up, went into the bathroom and started collecting my toiletries. When he said, "Don't leave" I had no answer for him as I walked out the door. Jude followed me to my car and all I could say was, "Go back to your wife." I drove away as fast as my little Ford Escort would take me. I was devastated. We had enjoyed each other so much. We had tons of fun, were compatible in every way, and had such a strong mutual attraction. Jude had only one flaw: he was married.

As I drove the two hours home, I cried my eyes out; I couldn't believe this was happening. My mind and heart were in total shock. This was before cell phones; my beeper was going off nonstop. It screamed all the way home.

The next day I couldn't concentrate at work. Being in a real estate office, one needs to be cheerful, happy, and cordial, but my heart was broken. Later that day the manager said I had a visitor in the lobby. Sure enough, it was Jude, sitting there, handsome as ever. He was in a three-piece suit and my guarded heart melted. He asked if he could take me to dinner and explain things. Part of me wanted to say,

"Explain what? You're married. Go back to your wife." I should have said that...but didn't.

At dinner his defense was, "Yes, I'm married but we have an agreement. I have a lot of money and I don't want to split it. She does what she wants. I do what I want. I'm not promising you anything but I know we can have a good time." I looked at him and made a conscious decision, rationalizing that it didn't matter if he was married. They had an agreement. Maybe she had a boyfriend, too. I was justifying my actions. That night Jude stayed in town at the local hotel. I went back and, for the first time, slept with him without my pajamas.

Being in MAP we make daily phone calls. I automatically woke up at five o'clock, snuck out of his bed and drove home to make my six a.m. phone call to my sponsor. Then I dialed information to get the number of the hotel. I wanted to let Jude know why I left without waking him. The phone number to the hotel was xxx-xxx-1666. I got such a spine-chilling feeling and knew without a shadow of a doubt that I had crossed the line. Sleeping with a married man was wrong, regardless of his arrangement. Seeing 666 just confirmed it. Again, I should have run for the hills but didn't. That was the beginning of my thirteen-year ordeal with Jude.

There are so many stories about Jude that I don't even know where to start. At the beginning it was a blast. I never had so much fun, but that's to be expected; when one is going downhill, life is easy. Looking back, the downward spiral is so obvious. In the midst of it, all I could see was excitement, exhilaration, and happiness while having the time of my life.

When I met Jude I was selling real estate to have extra money to travel. He started taking me everywhere. It soon became clear that we were traveling too much for me to concentrate on real estate, which was an eight-days-a-week-job. The exciting trips, the gifts and the cars were all extremely seductive. They were a great distraction from the fact that I was breaking one of the Commandments: *Thou Shall Not Commit Adultery*. I never admitted that he was still married. I conveniently repeated a half-truth saying he just wasn't divorced yet.

**Meeting at the Mailbox**

Renting out my rooms was the perfect solution to help me pay my bills. At the beginning it was easy to find women who wanted to live in my home. When I couldn't find women, men were eventually allowed in my house. Once I met Jude, that perfect solution changed. We met in September and within months we were going away at least every weekend and sometimes weeks at a time. Bert was an older man who watched over the house in my absence. He was a bit of a pushover and my house began to fall apart. It wasn't so much the physical ruin as much as the financial aspect of it.

After a year of traveling I put the house on the market but there were no offers. This was in the early nineties and a real estate bust was beginning. Since the house didn't sell and I didn't want it, Jude suggested that I stop paying the mortgage. He said to give it back to the bank, forcing me to lose my $15,000 down payment. Jude assured me that when I moved to New Hampshire he would buy me a condo.

My work in Massachusetts was very part-time and the flexibility was wonderful. It allowed me to come and go whenever I wanted. Months passed and foreclosure proceedings started. We had just come back from Colorado on the day that it was posted in the newspaper that my house would go up for auction. Bert and I were the only people living there. That day he had it all spiffed up because of my arrival home after a lengthy stay in Aspen. It was delightful to walk into my lovely home and have it so clean. It was just the way it always was before strangers started to live with me.

As I was walking to my mailbox the woman who owned the bungalow across the street was getting her mail, too. We had never met; she didn't live there, but had just done many renovations on the little house. I introduced myself and we started chatting. I asked her intentions for the house that used to be her mother's, who had recently passed away. She told me she wanted to sell it but wouldn't be able to for at least a year because of legal issues.

Suddenly the words came out of my mouth, "Would you be willing to rent it to me?" She expressed a little hesitancy because the house had just been completely renovated. I added, "Come into my house, see how I keep my home. I'm in the real estate business; a house will always sell faster if it's furnished." When she came into my house, she loved it. She immediately agreed that I would be a perfect tenant. Getting rent was better than leaving it vacant. Within an hour of my being back, the adorable bungalow right across the street would be my new home. Only God could have worked that out, only God. That would be my home for two years until it sold. It was perfect timing because after two years, New Hampshire was calling my name.

**Please Give Me a Townhouse**

I had been living in Nashua, New Hampshire, for a year when I went to a neighborhood party. The layout of the townhouse was adorable. It was small, sweet, efficient, and I wanted one. My rented garden style condo had been fine...until I saw the townhouse. From that moment my mission was to own one.

My investigation found that they were eight years old and had been purchased for $80,000. Their value was rising. Jude advised me to low-ball an offer to the existing owners. This development was two miles from my job and I usually went home for lunch. I always had a list of things to do during that hour. In the summer I loved to sit out on the patio to tan. There were only certain townhouses that would be perfect for tanning. The backyard needed to get direct sun at noon and could not be blocked by any shade. It couldn't be facing the main road and I needed privacy.

I strategically checked out the community. I taped notices on four doors in the front part of the development. The notice read, "I WANT TO BUY YOUR TOWNHOUSE. Cash Buyer. Please call Dyan," with my phone number. The next day two people called. One mentioned what they wanted for his home, which was way out of my price range. The other invited me over.

I made Jude's suggested offer of $20,000 cash. The owner kicked me out within seconds. Somewhat discouraged while relaying the outcome to Jude, he said not to worry. The townhouses were a dime a dozen and there were many more left. The next day I put my fliers on five more doors in a different area. I was now moving into the middle of the development. I received a call and skipped over to view another townhouse. I immediately was asked to leave when I presented my offer.

Jude was my cheerleader. He kept telling me to try again. He reminded me that somebody would want to sell, and $20,000 was all that they were worth. I continued my quest and when the seventh person had tossed me out I was totally defeated. I sat in my car and cried. "God, aren't You tired of me asking for a townhouse? Please, either give me my townhouse or take the desire out of my heart. Either way, I don't care, but I'm so tired of being rejected."

There was no place left to canvass except the back of the condo complex. I had already put my notices in all the other sections. I did not want to be in that area. God had a different plan.

The next day I went to the rear of the condo complex with tape and my notices. Three women were walking their baby carriages. I stopped them and pleaded, "Don't you know anyone who wants to sell? I really want to move here." One of the women said, "I think Donna's father is foreclosing, go ask her." She told me where Donna lived and I quickly drove over and knocked on the door. Thankfully, Donna was home and she gave me her father's phone number. I called him from the driveway and said, "I want to buy your townhouse. I will give you $20,000 cash." He replied, "I owe $40,000. I have $14,000. Can you come up with $26,000?" He heard me say without hesitation, "Yes, absolutely." I was over the moon!

I never went inside. It didn't matter. The carpets were going to be ripped up and anything that needed updating would be replaced. Everything would be painted white before move-in day. No home inspection and no bank appraisal were necessary. The real estate lawyer in my office building even gave me a discount. We all met two weeks later. With

44

my check for $26,000 and his check for $14,000, we signed the agreements. We paid off his obligation and I walked away with keys and the clean deed. No mortgage. I finally got my townhouse. Thank You, God. Thank You, God. Thank You, God.

After it was all said and done, the back of the complex is the best place to be. Isn't God amazing? He knew all along the perfect spot for me. No wonder the others didn't work out, this is where He wanted me. My big backyard is private, near the pool, with tons of parking, and my neighbors are wonderful. It's the nicest townhouse in the area and God gave it to me. Nobody believes this beautiful home was only $26,000.

**My God Can**

When I first started going to MAP we used a God Bag. It was a little brown paper bag with the word GOD on it. We wrote our worries, fears or desires on a piece of paper and put them in the bag, literally giving it to God. Years later, while I was on a MAP cruise, the gift shop was selling cute little boxes with GOD painted on them. They were adorable and so much better than a paper bag. I exclaimed my delight at these boxes. A little old woman standing next to me said, "It shouldn't be a box; it should be a can, because

GOD CAN." She was right, of course…God can! That year I made several "God Cans" for my family and friends. They were a hit and I still use mine today.

# CHAPTER 7 ~ CLOSE CALLS

*"They shall be mine"* says the Lord Almighty, *"in the day when I make up my treasured possession. I will spare them, just as in compassion a man spares his son who serves him."* ~ Malachi 3:17

## I Almost Died

Jude and I went elk hunting in Colorado every October. One year we rented horses. We also had a Jeep and a two-room tent at an elevation of almost 12,000 feet. Our morning routine started in the wee hours, some call it dark-thirty; it was still pitch black outside. The horses needed to be fed, which took forever because we didn't know what we were doing. We would ride them to our favorite areas and post, which meant sitting still for about an hour until dawn, waiting to see an elk. We would then saddle up and scope out other areas until early afternoon. We would eventually find our way back to camp, take a quick nap, and go out again just before dark.

One evening I was very tired and too cold to go out for that last run. Because it was freezing, I closed all the tent flaps, preventing any ventilation. I put a burner on for tea, while the other burner cooked our chicken. A lantern was fired up and the gas heater was on full blast. I was snug as a bug in a rug...a recipe for disaster in a tent.

Jude finally came back and we started eating. While getting up for more tea, my head started to spin. It felt like there was too much alcohol in my system, but I hadn't had a drink in years. I quickly sat down and was able to finish my meal. Our plan was to go down to check on our base camp, which was at the foot of the mountain, about an hour away. After dinner we shut everything off and as I walked out of the tent I collapsed. I had never passed out in my life. Jude heard the thud. As he picked me up he asked what was wrong. I hadn't a clue. While alert enough to stagger with assistance, I started to get sick in the Jeep. In my attempt to get out of the vehicle I didn't have the strength to open the door. Jude needed to help me. He thought it was food poisoning but this was way more serious than food poisoning. Gasping for air, hyperventilating, I couldn't get enough oxygen into my lungs, I could not breathe...and I couldn't move.

Jude wanted to put me back in the tent while he went down to base camp but I was still hyperventilating, too claustrophobic and certainly too sick to handle being inside. He propped me up against a tree stump as I continued to gasp for oxygen. Being semi-paralyzed, my arms and legs would not move but it didn't matter, I was more concerned about being able to breathe. I needed air...give me fresh air.

After what seemed like forever, the poison started to slowly leave my body. My head felt like mercury in a thermometer, going down in temperature, degree by degree. The whole time my mind was saying, "Thank You, God, my eyes are okay." A few minutes later, "Thank You, God, my nose is okay." Then "Thank You, God, my mouth is okay." I could feel the toxin seeping out of me inch by inch and clarity eventually came back. It was a slow process but I could definitely feel the difference. I went from almost dead, to being violently ill, and then just feeling sick. Without going into the gross details, fifteen pounds came out of my body that night. My entire insides were gone, just like when someone dies. I was that close to death.

Carbon monoxide poisoning is definitely a silent killer. I'm so thankful that I didn't fall into that death trap. Being outside in the frigid air and at 12,000 feet above sea level is what saved my life. God wasn't ready to take me yet.

## I Didn't Spill a Drop

The year after getting carbon monoxide poisoning, Jude and I decided to buy a small motor home for hunting. It was much more my style. We also traded in the horses for an ATV, making life much easier. We didn't have to wake up in the middle of the night to feed the ATV nor did it ever run away from us, like the horses did.

We shot out first trophy elk that year and couldn't wait to bring home our loot. We were towing a trailer containing several hundred pound coolers filled to the brim with elk meat and dry ice. We were on an urgent mission to get back to New Hampshire as fast as possible.

It was almost dusk and it had been raining. We were driving a little too fast for the slick conditions. As we entered Hartford, Connecticut there was a bad hairpin turn. Coming into that unexpected spot we saw that the traffic ahead had stopped. As Jude was trying to brake I could feel the trailer behind us start to fishtail; there was not enough room to stop. The only thing I could repeat out loud was, "Please Jesus, please Jesus, please Jesus, please Jesus." Jude just said, "Hold on, I'm going to aim for the biggest vehicle. We are definitely going to hit something." There were four or five lanes of traffic so we smashed into a big van, which then put us perpendicular to the traffic. In an instant, our trailer had jackknifed into our motor home. I was watching in terror as the oncoming cars were aiming at us. A car hit us and the domino effect bounced us into two more cars. Although six cars were totaled in this accident, I never spilled a drop of coffee from my cup. It was nothing short of a miracle that no one was hurt.

Jude received a $70 traffic violation for going too fast for the roadway conditions. He had been complaining to Ford Motor Company about problems with the motor home brakes. He was able to fight the ticket by claiming that it was the fault of the brakes, not of his driving capabilities. He won the court case and his fine was dismissed. He was also reimbursed for his expenses for his nine-month old motor home. As I often said, Jude had two brains but no heart, especially when it concerned money. Jude was the ultimate, cunning, exaggerating opportunist. If there was a money angle or someone to take advantage of financially, he would find it. Thus began the start of my questioning his integrity while denying that anything was wrong.

## The Truck on the Hill

My first brush with death was in kindergarten when Mrs. Hebert was bringing me and her son to school. She was driving up a steep and narrow hill to go over Thatcher Street Bridge. There was a big truck in front of us. Suddenly the back doors of that truck broke loose. Monstrous wooden spools rolled out and bounced towards us. We had no place to go. In a nanosecond she put the car in reverse. She was able to back onto a scant strip of land on the side of the hill in an attempt to escape the giant cylinders. The out-of-control spools spiraled past us, as we watched in shock. It was quite a scary experience for a five-year-old to witness.

There was only one spot on that hill for us to back into. We were at that exact location the instant those potentially deadly spools broke loose. Had we been anywhere else on that hill, we would not have escaped. Those wooden giants would have smashed into the windshield. They would have caused injury for sure, perhaps even killing us. I can now see that I have always been protected.

## Palm Sunday

It was my senior year in high school. My parents, my sister, Nancy, and I were going to visit a college where I had been accepted. Since my Uncle Hal owned a plane, we decided to fly for an hour or two instead of drive for five hours on a beautiful clear Palm Sunday. We were excited to be taking this trip and stopped by my father's car wash before we left for the small, local airport. My brother Mike was working there that day. As we said our goodbyes, my mother said to my brother, "If anything happens to us, take care of Patty." It was eight o'clock in the morning and my eyes started to fill up. What a horrible thought.

The flight there was uneventful; flying was certainly faster and more enjoyable than driving. The college campus was scenic. We had a delicious lunch, and while we were at the airport, Nancy bought candy bars and put them in her purse. When we were ready to head home, we took our seats inside the plane. My uncle was in the pilot seat and I was beside him. My father was behind me, next to my mother, and my sister was sitting in the back, sideways. It looked like a little jump seat.

We were soon airborne and cruising. I turned around and yelled over the roar of the engines, "Nan, can I have that PayDay?" My father jumped out of his seat and repeated what he thought he heard, "Mayday?" Mayday is a word used internationally as a distress signal. It's used for a life-threatening emergency. "No, Dad, not Mayday. PayDay. PayDay is a candy bar." We all got a good laugh at my Dad's expense.

The view is amazing when you're flying in a small aircraft. We were only 6,500 feet up. It was my first time in a plane and it was lovely. We were in a five-seater, single engine Cessna, so it was extremely loud but we were able to yell above the noise. You actually get used to the sound...until it stops.

It was such a strange sensation; the silence was deafening. The altimeter was now going backwards. My father frantically asked my uncle what was happening, and his reply was a concerned, "I don't know. Put your seat belts on." After I buckled mine, Hal asked me to hold the wheel, which is called the yoke, while he put his seat belt on. I was a senior in high school, had just received my driver's license, and thought it would be like driving a car. I was wrong. When my uncle let go of his yoke, the wheel that I was holding was immediately sucked up into the dashboard. We did a nosedive. It felt like we were going down a steep roller coaster, only we were not. We were in a plane headed directly towards the ground. My uncle grabbed his yoke and it yanked us out of the fall and pointed us in the opposite direction, up. If we were ever going to puke that would have been the time. Both actions were abrupt and severe.

My father was clearly panicking, screaming, "Hal, what's happening?" My uncle then repeated the word that had been said minutes before. He was now speaking into his radio, "Mayday-Mayday-Mayday."

My ears were exploding. The first thought that came into my mind was, "We can't be crashing; I'm going to college next year." My sister was crying and my mother was hysterical. My father was nervously calling out the altimeter readings every hundred feet we dropped. "Hal, we're at 2200 feet. Hal, we're at 2100 feet. Hal, where are you going to land? Where are you going to put this plane?" My head felt like it was going to burst because we were free-falling fast. I kept on silently screaming a prayer in my head, "Please Jesus, please Jesus, please Jesus." I was also saying *The Lord's Prayer* as fast as I could. Then I started to laugh because it all seemed so surreal.

Hal finally reached somebody on the radio at an airport near Boston. Air Traffic Control could see us on their radar and they told Hal what degrees to position the flaps, which slowed our descent. Hal kept reassuring us, "Don't worry. If we have to, we will belly up into the trees. Don't worry, if we have to, we will land on the highway, facing the traffic. Don't worry. Don't worry."

We were able to land on the emergency strip of an airport just outside of Boston. The ambulance and fire trucks came out in full alarm fanfare. Ironically, the landing with no power was smoother than the landing we had with power. We were safe. We made it. Hanscom Field has several obstructions. We were told that if we were one hundred feet further away or one hundred feet lower we would not have made it.

What really did happen to the plane to make the engine die forty minutes into our flight home? We ran out of gas! There were two full gas tanks when we left in the morning and we used three-quarters of one of them for the flight up. Before we left to fly home, Hal switched over to the full tank. Sometime after liftoff it was flipped back. We were flying on the quarter of a tank remaining from our original flight. When we had used all the gas from the first tank, the engine simply stopped.

Sixty-five hundred feet up in the air is no place to run out of gas, especially if there is a full tank of fuel right beside the empty tank. My uncle was calm and thorough in all his control checking. He was pulling knobs and doing everything he could think of while we were plummeting. He never once checked the gas. When I repeat this story to any pilot they are always appalled. Hal did not follow *The Emergency Checklist*. Hal missed the first thing to troubleshoot if there is loss of engine power: check fuel gauge.

Other than for a brief moment, the fear of death did not enter my mind. College was in my immediate future, as silly as that sounds. My mother's comment to my brother as we left, however, was haunting. Did she have a mother's premonition that something was going to happen? We relive this experience every Palm Sunday and we call each other if we are not together. After that ordeal it was decided I was not going to the college five hours away. I would attend a school that was an hour north of my home. Once again, the hand of God was protecting me and my family. Thank You, God.

## The Warthog

Another near death experience was in Africa. Jude was an expert marksman and he loved to hunt. We traveled extensively in the United States and Canada, and were making plans to go hunting in Alaska when we met a couple in Aspen who suggested that we go to Africa instead. "In Alaska you hunt the animals. In Africa, the animals hunt you back."

It was the trip of a lifetime, spending three weeks in Africa on a hunting safari. We ended up going with the couple from Aspen, although I had a strong dislike for the man. Rudolph was a user, a taker, and would go out of his way to not pay for things; he was not my type of guy. Since Jude was a generous man it didn't seem to bother him but it irked me. Rudolph's wife was the exact opposite. She was just as sweet as he was greedy. I was thrilled to learn that they would be hunting with another group.

The safari group had given us strict instructions before leaving the United States. We could only bring two of everything: two pairs of shorts, two tops, two sweatshirt s, two pairs of pants, etc. What we wore one day was hand-washed and stone pressed the following day while we were hunting. The fabulously laundered clothes would be left in our hut. The netting over our bed protected us from the huge, seven-inch furry black spiders that lived in the thatched roof. Creepy.

One day we were hunting with our regular team: the estate owner, two guides, Jude and me. Occasionally we would see a warthog, an ugly, obese cousin to the pig. The guides kept telling us to wait for a massive hog. Since these were African animals and we had no idea what we were looking for, we trusted our leaders. Everyone carried a gun except me. This day we were semi-spread out, not hunting in our usual close unison formation. They saw a huge warthog, someone yelled, "Shoot him!" Jude got a quick shot off but it only hit the animal in the rear. The hog immediately did a complete turn around and headed right for me. My first thought was to climb the nearby tree, only to find it was a thorn tree with four-inch spikes. In horror, I turned to face the warthog as he charged within ten feet of me. He then took a ninety-degree right-hand turn and went running through the reeds. It was as if he ran into a glass wall and he couldn't get any closer to me...it was nothing short of a miracle. Since the hog was injured, it didn't take long for the guys to find him. When they dragged him out, the estate owner took a blade of grass and went underneath the tusk. It was razor sharp and it sliced the reed in two. The hog would have torn me to shreds.

They told me later that because I was in the direct line of fire with the warthog that everyone was too afraid to shoot. I am so grateful for that invisible glass, or an angel, or whatever it was that made him veer off so abruptly. The picture that was taken with this trophy warthog captured an elated gal who was happy to be alive.

# CHAPTER 8 ~ TAKING BACK MY LIFE

*"For we wrestle not against flesh and blood, but against principalities, against powers, against the rulers of the darkness of this world, against spiritual wickedness in high places."* ~ Ephesians 6:12

## I Know You Don't Want to Split Your Money

Jude and I had been traveling, golfing, skiing, biking, hiking, hunting, kayaking, snowshoeing, grilling, buying or selling cars and motor homes, and anything else we wanted to do. One day I woke up and it was our ten-year anniversary. We had been dating for a decade. It hit me that we could continue doing this forever but I wanted more; I wanted a commitment and that was not possible with Jude.

On the day of our anniversary we were in Florida golfing and partying. I got the courage to tell him, "I understand that you don't want to split your money, but I don't want to be a girlfriend when I'm sixty-five years old. It's been a wonderful ten years with you, the best years of my life, but I am moving on." Jude was shocked; he didn't think I was serious. I felt good about my decision; it was solid and right. There were no emotional goodbyes when I got on the plane to fly back to New Hampshire. It was time for me to get on with my life.

Within weeks Jude started to backpedal. He said he didn't want to lose me and that he would get a divorce. He started looking for diamonds. I was surprised, yet thrilled.

Two weeks later I headed back to Tampa with a connection through Cincinnati. The weatherman predicted an early snowstorm. The flight attendant came on the plane. She said, "Because we need so much deicer, fifteen of you have to get off the plane. Or you can all stay on, but no luggage will be able to go. You decide amongst yourselves, but we cannot go with everyone and the luggage," and then she left. I felt like we were on the show *Survivor*. My defense to the people around me was, "I'm getting engaged. I have to stay on the plane." Everyone seemed to have their own compelling reason why they, too, needed to remain.

It was clear that no one was willing to leave the plane. There was a couple seated near me who also needed to get to Tampa. We decided that we would take our chances with the Boston shuttle the airline offered. The three of us got off the plane, collected our luggage, and hopped in the taxi. We bolted to Boston as fast as the driver dared to go, in an attempt to beat the approaching storm. At Boston a jet to Tampa was leaving in fifteen minutes and there was one seat left. I looked at the couple. They didn't want to separate and said I should take it. It ended up arriving only twenty minutes later than my original connecting flight. The New Hampshire plane never left because the people couldn't agree on who would get kicked off. The snow ultimately grounded them.

Jude was waiting for me in Tampa. He had a big smile, a stunning four-carat diamond ring, and a promise of divorce. I had never been happier. Although Jude seemed happy too, I think he started to feel the pressure of now having to make a drastic lifestyle change. He started acting like a caged animal.

The ring appeased me for a while. Ten months later the tragedy of 9/11 happened. My company announced a headcount reduction; I was first to volunteer. For the next eighteen months we traveled all over the United States and Canada in a luxury motor home. The only thing we needed to do every winter day was to decide whether we would ski, snowshoe or cross-country ski. In the nicer weather would we golf, bike, hike, hunt, or kayak? Life was full of activity, but no real purpose. I rarely saw my family although we talked on the phone all the time. The MAP program was still important to me. It was difficult with Jude since he thought it was ridiculous that I didn't eat sugar or flour. It particularly bothered him that I didn't consume alcohol. He wanted a drinking buddy for his nightly martini. He would give me a hard time when I wanted to go to MAP meetings while we were traveling. This behavior inspired another mantra of mine: I get more support from my pantyhose than I do from Jude. Everyone always laughed when I said it, but it was a sad truth. Jude even thought I was stupid for interrupting our ski trip in Salt Lake City to fly home for my grandmother's ninetieth birthday party. I was appalled. He would have walked a thousand miles if he had the opportunity to see his deceased grandmother again. My grandmother was still here. Shame on him for trying to discourage me from participating in such a momentous occasion.

One of the reasons that we lasted so long was because I stood up to Jude. Many people didn't. They were so enamored by the fact that he had money, they would bend over backwards trying to appease him. I didn't take any guff from him; I would stand firm, stick to my guns and defend myself. Although he complained, it was obvious that he respected me.

As mentioned before, I questioned his integrity around many areas. Money seemed to be his god; Jude worshiped the almighty dollar. Although we didn't go to church, I never got into bed at night without getting on my knees. I always said my prayers and thanked God for my day. I never started my day without getting on my knees, asking God for help. Occasionally Jude would say, "Put in a good word for me," which I gladly did.

It was after the engagement that Jude started to be more critical of me. For some reason it irked him if I was doing a good deed. He hated to see me help someone, compliment someone, or even return a shopping cart. Anything that looked like an act of kindness would irritate him. He was the first one to remind me that the people we were talking to at the restaurant or ski resorts were not my friends. We had just met them – I didn't have to be friendly to them because I'd never see them again. He would try to demean and almost bully me. I could never understand why he was so critical of me for being nice.

Jude grew up as the Golden Child. He was the first-born, gifted in every way. He had good looks, a quick brain, an athletic body, business savvy, and a charming personality. He had the attitude that rules were meant for everyone except him – he was entitled. Once he became wealthy, there was no stopping him. He took whatever he wanted, whenever he wanted. If he couldn't get "something" then that would become his new quest. He just had to have that unattainable object. He loved a challenge and his motto was, "The fun of the hunt, the thrill of the kill."

I was talking with my friend Linda about how Jude was becoming more judgmental. I jokingly mentioned that he probably sold his soul for money. Upon hearing those words out loud, an eerie feeling overcame me and I said with fright, "Oh my God, he did. He sold his soul. What does he want with me?" It took a few seconds for it to register but I heard myself say, "Oh no…he's after mine! He's after my soul." I had a sick feeling in the pit of my stomach that made me want to throw up. Did I just hit upon an evil truth? The thought was somewhat terrifying and every day Jude did something to reinforce it.

**The Angels and The Devils**

There were many events that led up to this evening I'm about to describe. It was an accumulation of numerous situations that just deteriorated. Jude was hypercritical and extremely judgmental. Every minute away from him I spent planning how to end the relationship. My courage seemed to melt away in the presence of his demanding and controlling personality.

We had been engaged for three years. His upcoming divorce was going so slowly it probably was never going to happen. I said to him one night, "If I died tomorrow I'd probably go to hell. I'm breaking the Seventh Commandment, *Thou Shall Not Commit Adultery*." Jude just shook his head and said in a real nasty voice, "I feel sorry for you. I can't believe you even think there's a heaven or a hell." When he said that my stomach felt sick and I could almost see the horns on his head. I should have left immediately but did not. On my way home the next night I was in conflict. I was disgusted with myself for not having the courage to end this unhealthy relationship.

My friend Peter rented my townhouse for one and a half years while Jude and I travelled. We had just recently returned from yet another trip. Peter was still in the spare bedroom and I was in my master bedroom with a deadbolt on my door.

That night at 3:26 I woke up needing to use the bathroom. I didn't want to get out of my cozy bed but I did want to stay awake seven more minutes to see 3:33 on the clock. I waited under my covers.

Suddenly I heard someone run up the stairs. It was a little late for Peter or his son, who occasionally stayed over, to be running up the stairway. Then I heard wrestling. Have you ever heard people wrestling? They're not talking, they're not screaming, it's more like grunting and groaning. Well, that's what I heard outside my door. By this time I was sitting up in bed, looking in the direction of the hallway on the other side of my door. I was wondering what they were doing. Then the shrieking started, a noise that I had never heard before. It sounded like a cat being stabbed. It seemed to get angrier, more violent, and increasingly louder. The pitch was horrible and scary. My back was pressed hard against my headboard as I tried to get away from the terrifying noise. I was petrified. This was not an earthly sound. Whatever it was, it was enraged, and I was unbelievably frightened. I was frantically praying that whatever it was would not come through the door. It seemed like it went on forever and then it just quit. The evil screeching simply stopped. I was paralyzed in my bed, terrified to my core, and had no idea what had just happened.

I immediately felt in my spirit and heard in my soul, *"Enough is enough. I want you to realize what's really at stake here; your soul is in jeopardy. That was the Angels and the devils fighting over your soul. You choose, but I want you to know that your soul is in jeopardy."*

It was the scariest moment in my entire life. I couldn't even talk about it without violently shaking and crying hysterically. That morning my MAP people did not call, which was very unusual. Peter usually slept until eight but was up at six-thirty and sitting in the living room. That was also out of the ordinary. Between my sobs and hysteria I tried to tell Peter what happened. He hadn't heard anything during the night.

The next thing I did was call Jude and told him I couldn't see him anymore. Trying to repeat what had happened just hours earlier sounded crazy as the words came out of my mouth. I knew every one of them was true. He tried to convince me that it was a nightmare. He finally said, "You're breaking up with me over a flipping dream?" My tearful response was, "It was not a dream. I wish it were." It was real and it scared me straight.

Later that day I had lunch with my friend Sheila. During my hysteria and tears she said, "That was good versus evil outside your door. How would you like to listen to *that* for eternity?"

It was hours later when I realized it was September 24, thirteen years to the day that Jude and I met. When God says, "*Enough is enough,*" you know it's over. I never went back to Jude. It took what it took to get me away from him. God knew it had to be something huge, something terrifying, to give me the courage. Later that night I searched my daily readings for some sort of explanation. "No one would ever sin if their eyes would be unveiled and they could see how their slips delight the evil spirits."

My eyes were not unveiled but my ears were. I was able to hear this battle, the battle over my soul.

*"We wrestle not against flesh and blood, but against principalities, against powers, against the rulers of the darkness of this world, against spiritual wickedness in high places."* Ephesians 6:12.

I heard those principalities wrestle over my soul. I'm so grateful the Angels won. It took months for me to retell this without crying and reliving the terror. This happened many years ago and it still chills me.

**How to Pray**

My friend Debbie told me about a seminar on "How to Pray" that sounded intriguing. It was being held at one of the prettiest churches in Nashua. My interest was also curiosity since I had never been inside that church. Unfortunately, the session was in a large classroom, not in the Chapel. At the end of the seminar, the instructor was telling a story of when he went to a monastery for a weekend of prayer. He said that between five in the evening and five in the morning everyone would be in their individual rooms, taking the vow of silence. It was the prayer before they all went to their respective rooms that caught my attention. "Protect us from the evil spirits that roam the hallways at night."

Because of my experience with the Angels and the devils a thought crossed my mind. "Does this happen every evening, everywhere, to everyone?" On that particular evening I was able to hear those evil spirits that roamed my hallway at night.

## CHAPTER 9 ~ CLICKING WITH GOD

*"Jesus said, 'I have told you these things, so that in me you may have peace.' "* ~ John 16:33

### Have You Ever Heard the Voice of God?

Soon after Jude and I broke up, my niece, Ivy, introduced me to online dating. One of my first dates was with a pleasant gentleman. Although there was no romantic interest, I enjoyed his company and our interesting conversation. Before we even had dinner, out of nowhere, he asked, "Have you ever heard the Voice of God?" It took me by such surprise because it was so out of context. We weren't even talking about God or spirituality. I simply answered, "Yes, have you?" He continued to tell me that years before he had fallen off a roof and was in the hospital waiting for emergency surgery. That's when he heard God say, *"Don't worry, you will be all right."* He was.

It made me think of the times that I had heard God's Voice. By hearing somebody else speak it, it became clear. When I talk about myself I use the first person singular pronoun 'I'. I never talk about myself in the second person singular, 'You'. This was the first time that I made that connection. My date didn't hear "I will be all right" because it wasn't him talking. Somebody outside of himself was saying, *"You will be all right."* Just as in all the times I had heard

God speak to me, He always said, "*You*". It clearly was an outside, audible voice and it definitely was not mine.

## Tithing to Kathleen

Tithing, giving a tenth of what is earned, was not actively practiced in my church. It is a huge sign of faith. Kathleen had been the recipient of my tithe money because I knew she needed it more than the church. We had met when Rick and I first moved to Boston. I lost track of Kathleen for several years while I was gallivanting around the country with Jude. I always assumed that she was getting along fine in Boston.

After the split with Jude I started going back to church. I usually went with my friend Christine. One day she left her pocketbook in the car and only took a dollar for the collection basket. I must have given her a questioning look because she said to me, "Why, how much do you give?" My thoughts quickly went back to Kathleen. I told Christine, "I used to tithe my money to my friend Kathleen." I hadn't seen her for quite a while so I took my 10% and dropped it into the basket.

You can imagine my delight and surprise when I received a phone call from Kathleen that evening. My gladness soon turned to major concern. She told me she was helpless, homeless, living on the streets, and destitute. I was horrified for her.

I called the bus company, paid for a ticket, and early the next day she was on her way to stay with me. That didn't work out very well for a variety of reasons. She was soon on a bus back to Boston but at least she had money in her pocket.

## King

While I was dating online I also heard about MM.com. It sounded intriguing so I enrolled for three months. I preferred to date men who lived within twenty-five miles of my home but there were often interesting men who lived outside that radius. On MM.com there were many who were willing to hop on a plane and have a dinner date in New England. King was one of them.

My rule on Internet dating was simple. We email back and forth two or three times and if there was a connection, then we would talk on the phone two or three times. Most matches didn't even progress to the phone stage. If it seemed that there was a possibility of a potential relationship then we would meet.

King was from Ohio. He passed the general guidelines so we made plans for him to visit me. I picked him up at Logan Airport in Boston, forty-five minutes away from my home and he stayed at one of the lovely waterfront hotels. It was summertime and the city was alive with excitement and festivities. We had a great afternoon visiting all the tourist attractions. In the evening we went to the

North End where they were celebrating one of their many feasts. We ate at a cozy café and danced under the moonlit sky while the band played on the outside stage. I returned the next day for brunch and then brought King back to Logan. It was a quick but awesome rendezvous.

Since my birthday was two weeks away, he offered to take me to one of the resorts on Lake Erie. I took him up on it, along with the stipulation we would have separate rooms. We immediately booked a flight and started making plans to celebrate my birthday in Ohio. It sounded like fun to me. My family vehemently disagreed.

I have been blessed with a free and trusting spirit. I take everything at face value. Unless I have a reason to doubt, it doesn't enter my mind to question. That's neither smartest nor safest way to live...or date.

Hopping on a plane to spend the weekend with a man I didn't even know was probably not a good idea. All I saw was fun, adventure and excitement. One by one my family members called and tried to get me to think logically. My sister, Pat, said that she was concerned for my safety; I assured her that King was a gentleman. My sister, Nancy, said that if anything happened to me, our family would be devastated. I defended my position, claiming that it was only for a weekend and I'd be fine. My mom called and said she didn't want me to go. Period. "Ma," was my only comment to her and I quickly changed the subject.

It wasn't until my friend Kathleen expressed sheer terror for my safety that I started to reconsider the trip. Since Kathleen did not have a phone, I could only talk to her when she called me. It was interesting that she should contact me so soon after the calls from my concerned family members. It was how she opened the conversation that grabbed my attention. She was so relieved that I answered the phone. She said she had this horrible premonition about me. When I assured her that all was fine and shared my upcoming travel intentions she became frantic. "You can't go. This is why I'm calling. You won't come back. He has bodies buried on his property. You can't go." She was hysterical in her pleading. While trying to calm her down, my mind started to be open to the possibility that King might not be the sweet person I envisioned. Other than a day in Boston and a few phone calls and emails, I really didn't know anything about him. Kathleen then suggested I call my ex-husband, a DEA Agent, to ask him to do a background check on this man who called himself King.

Minutes later King called. He asked if I was all ready for the approaching weekend with him. I repeated my family's concern and King condescendingly said, "You're a big girl. You can make your own decisions." I nonchalantly mentioned Kathleen's suggestion of having my ex-husband do a quick background check. King flipped and went ballistic. He lost all composure and a nasty, bullying side of him came out. He started to badger me about making up my own mind. I shouldn't listen to others. I should do what I want to do. I already said I was going. While I listened to him rant on, this dreadful feeling in the pit of my stomach started to brew. This was the real King and I knew then that I didn't care to find out any more about him. I would not be getting on that plane.

When we hung up the phone I continued the thought of asking Rick to check out this guy, King, who just went from sweet to nasty in five seconds. Not the characteristic of a sane or stable man. My concern turned to terror as I opened my computer to look up Rick's phone number. The MSN home page featured a story titled "Where Are All the Missing Girls?" Pictures of lost girls were staring me straight in the face and I was chilled to the bone. It was a huge confirmation that I would have been in real danger had I gone on that adventure. The strangest thing about that day was when I went back later to read that MSN article, it was nowhere to be found. Nowhere. God was protecting me when He sent me my sisters, my mom, and Kathleen. He eventually showed me the pictures of all the missing girls that were on the screen, for my eyes only.

## I Recognize Those Ski Boots

One and a half years after I broke up with Jude, my sister, Nancy, invited me to join her skiing while she attended a seminar in Colorado. We had just finished our last run of the day. As we were taking off our skis some man rudely skied so close he could have hit us. I recognized those ski boots. I waited until the skier stopped and then yelled, "Jude." He turned around and looked in my direction. Even from a distance I could tell the shock, disbelief, and then total joy at seeing me. Since my sister and I were on our way to have coffee I invited him to join us, my treat. He kiddingly replied, "That's a first!" We went in and three cups of coffee cost $6.66 and I freaked. Nancy tossed in a pack of gum to change the total of the bill. I felt God saying real loud and clear, "*Don't even think about it.*" It was a great reminder why I was not with him anymore. My soul had been in jeopardy and it could easily be again. We had our coffee and parted ways. Thanks for the reminder, God.

## It's Not Rejection

I have always wanted a special man in my life. I got picked to be Sleeping Beauty in kindergarten because I was the only girl who would kiss a boy, the Prince. I even had a boyfriend in second grade. Being boy crazy would be part of my life until just recently; now I've been focusing on my family and my entrepreneurship.

Two things carried me through most of the breakups, bad matches and jerks, lack of chemistry, disappointments, close calls and heartaches.

A favorite saying is *"It's not Rejection, it's Divine Protection."* The other is from an unknown author of Perfect Love, where God says, *"I want you to stop planning and stop wishing. Allow me to bring that person to you. You just keep watching me, expecting the greatest things."* This is great advice which I need to have imprinted in my brain. It's comforting when I remember it. Unfortunately I often try to make it happen instead of letting it happen.

## You Can Leave Now

I had worked at The Control Place (TCP) for over a year and disliked it almost every day. There was some sort of evil spirit in that company. The management was vicious, mean, and hateful. Most of the employees were wonderful, but the office manager and the facilities manager had serious streaks of nasty. I had never experienced anything like that before. Several times I spoke to both of them separately, and repeatedly asked if I had done anything to offend them. They both claimed there was absolutely nothing wrong but they continued to treat me with contempt. It was obvious to everyone, even though both blatantly denied it. My good friend Linda and I were talking one day and behind me, in the distance, was the office manager. Linda looked at me and said, "I know why Frita hates you." "Why? Why is she so mean to me?" "She's jealous. It is so clear, she's a fat mess and you are not." I'm not sure how accurate that observation was but there was nothing I could do to get Frita to be civil to me. I started to look for new job.

I landed the perfect position with ISO and would be starting the second week in January. ISO had no problem with me taking a week off in March to go skiing in Aspen. Since TCP required a two week notice, it would coincide with my going back to work after the Christmas holiday.

On January 2, management received my resignation letter. When I went to TCP that morning the owner called me into his office. He said that they didn't need me any longer and that I could leave at the end of the day. "Are you firing me?" I asked incredulously. "We don't need you anymore," was his angry reply. He was cutting his nose to spite his face because there was so much to do with the start of a new year. There were definitely two weeks of work needed to update everything. Now he was telling me he wanted me to work just one day. I'm not quite sure how the words came out of my mouth. I heard myself say, "If you're letting me go at the end of the day, I'd just as soon leave now." I grabbed my things, trying to hold back tears. It felt like I had just been fired rather than them honoring my resignation. I was in shock.

It was not even nine in the morning. The first thing I did was call the Office of Unemployment. They reassured me that I could collect benefits for two weeks because TCP laid me off. I did not have to search for employment since I would start working in two weeks at my new position. That seemed to ease the blow. My next call was to my friend Laurie in Aspen, whose first question was, "When are you coming out here?" My excited reply was, "Tomorrow."

I used frequent flyer miles for my March ticket so I was able to just switch the date. Within twenty-four hours my bags were packed and I was on my way to Aspen. My postcard to TCP was a stunning view of a snow-covered mountain and in my perfect penmanship I wrote: *"I'm in Aspen skiing. What a glorious surprise to be here instead of working. God is great and I love being on His winning team! ~ Dyan"*

My friends at the office were thrilled for me. I'm sure the nasty management disliked me even more. I was happy to be in Aspen and even happier to be out of TCP. I was especially grateful for having an early vacation, two weeks in Aspen instead of one, and for not needing to take any vacation time in March.

## Homeless Millionairess

A few months before Kathleen's desperate visit to me, she was befriended by a wealthy man. He left her three million dollars in his will. She was on disability at the time. There is a disclaimer on disability checks that states if you receive any inheritance, win the lottery or get a job you must report it. Failure to report a change of income constitutes fraud. It carries penalties ranging from loss of benefits to imprisonment. Kathleen was worried about getting thrown in jail. She immediately went down to the state office to show them the documents. They were happy for her. They immediately stopped her benefits, which would be the logical course of action.

That was over thirteen years ago; Kathleen has not received her inheritance yet. She is no longer eligible to receive disability so she is worse off than she has ever been. I call her my homeless millionairess friend. It's pitiful. There are times that she doesn't even have a dollar in her pocket. But she stands to eventually inherit millions. The spouse of the man who left Kathleen the inheritance told her, "Oh no, Dear, you will only get the money upon my passing." That woman is now 103 years old and is still going strong. She repeatedly tells Kathleen to trust Jesus.

## The Woman Bending Down

In the meantime, to make life simple for Kathleen, I opened a bank account with both our names on it so I could get money to her on a regular basis. This was the only solution because she had no home address to receive mail. Many times when Kathleen went into the bank she felt like she was being attacked by demons. Once she even closed out not just our joint account but also all my personal accounts. You can imagine my hysteria when I checked online and everything had a zero balance. The bank was able to reverse this error but it put me into a real panic.

Because Kathleen did not have a phone there was no way for me to contact her, she would always have to call me. Weeks had gone by since she had closed our account. It was impossible to get any money to her.

One gorgeous evening I was in Boston for a Red Sox game with my friend Dave and his two sons. I don't normally have much cash with me. That night I had money tucked away in my pocketbook, just in case. Before the game we ate at a wonderful restaurant in the North End of Beantown. As we were walking to the subway through a construction area detour I almost stepped on a woman who was bending down tying her boot. I stopped until she finished. Who do you think this woman was? You guessed it: Kathleen. What are the chances, with hundreds of people on that detour, with thousands of people going to the Red Sox game and half a million people living in Boston, that I would almost bump into Kathleen? What are the chances that she would be bending down and I would be courteous enough not to run into her like many people were?

You can imagine my delight when she stood up. She was so happy to see me, too, and I was thrilled to be able to give her some cash. It's so heartwarming to be able to help someone out, to really make a difference. Both my sisters have helped me out in the past, too, and I am forever grateful to them. Thank You, God, for my wonderful sisters. I am blessed.

I'm sure there are lessons to be learned here. Kathleen is being more responsible, not only for her finances, what little she has, but also her actions. Last year she won $20,000 on a scratch ticket so she rented a room at the YWCA and paid for an entire year. Unfortunately, the year has expired. Although she is not on the street yet, every day she is threatened with the fear of eviction. Financially, I cannot help her as much as I did years ago, but she still receives money from me on a not-so-regular basis. She promises to pay me back when she comes into her inheritance. That will be wonderful if she does, but if I don't get paid back in this lifetime, it will come in the next. That's okay. God is watching.

## Jack Canfield

My three friends and I went to a Jack Canfield seminar. He spoke about many topics from his *Chicken Soup for the Soul* series. Jack's mentor, W. Clement Stone, had a personal connection with one of my friends. Jan's ex-husband married Mr. Stone's secretary. Stone bought his secretary a house, and upon his death her mortgage was paid in full. He also left her $1 million but there was a hitch. The secretary did not receive the money at the time of Stone's death. She only inherited it after his wife passed away, which was eight years later. I was happy to hear this story and could not wait to relay this message to Kathleen. Somebody else had been in her exact situation. Not wishing for someone to pass, but having to wait until they died to receive an inheritance. I often remind Kathleen that soon she will be a millionairess and all these difficulties will be forgotten. She will never have to worry about money again. She is a spiritual person but she vacillates between belief and panic. I believe God has kept us together for over thirty years so I can encourage her to have faith and not fear.

## CHAPTER 10 ~ I BELIEVE

*"This man came to Jesus by night and said, 'Rabbi, we know that you are a teacher who has come from God. For no one could perform the miraculous signs you are doing if God were not with him.' " ~ John 3:2*

### Believe Book

My friend Janet bought me a beautiful book about Angels titled *Believe*. It is delightful with gorgeous paintings of Angels and wonderful poetry. The cherub on the front cover is precious and adorable. It's in my hallway on my hope chest, the same area where the Angels and the devils were wrestling.

I was upstairs one evening and shut off the lights thinking that my bedroom light was still on. It wasn't. You can imagine my surprise when the only thing visible in my dark hallway was *B E L I E V E*. It was the iridescent paint on the book cover. God was giving me a *God-wink* telling me to BELIEVE. I often retell this story to visitors in my home and I love showing them what happens to the book once the lights are out. Everyone reacts the same way: "WOW." I love my book. I Believe.

### Dragonfly

My co-worker Cathy was talking about doing a writing meditation. She would place a pen and paper next to her while meditating.

Instead of trying to dismiss intruding thoughts she wrote them down to share them with others. It sounded like an interesting exercise. One morning a huge dragonfly was near my car. I hadn't seen a dragonfly in years. I immediately thought of butterflies, and butterflies always reminded me of God. I raised my eyes and just smiled.

When I went to work that day Cathy told me she did a writing meditation the night before. She asked if she could share it with me. I couldn't wait to hear. She went through her list. She said everything made sense except the last entry: dragonfly. She had no idea what dragonfly meant. I just smiled and said, "That's for me. I saw a huge dragonfly this morning and thought of God, so it was my little *God-wink*."

In my mail that evening was a movie from Netflix titled "Dragonfly". God was smiling on me that day as He gave me a double *God-wink*.

## I'll Be Your Personal Trainer

As I've mentioned before, I'm compulsive about almost everything…except housework and exercise. While dating Jude, we exercised all the time. We were very active with skiing, biking, snowshoeing, golf, and hunting. Anything to keep us moving.

Now that we were not dating I needed to work out on my own, and that reality did not thrill me.

My friend Kelli mentioned that she had paid eleven hundred dollars for a nutritionist. My thought was, "Good for you. I'm in MAP and have a food plan of no flour, no sugar, and no alcohol. I don't need a nutritionist." When she added that she also hired a personal trainer, I got a twinge of envy. She mentioned the coach was even more expensive than the nutritionist. I knew it was out of my price range. I quickly dismissed it…until the following week.

The conversation with Kelli flashed back in my head. I pouted, "I wish that I had extra money for personal trainer. A workout buddy would help me stick to a routine." That's when I heard God say, *"I'll be your personal trainer. I won't charge you sixteen hundred dollars. I won't take vacations. I won't forget you. I'll show up every day."* I just laughed and shook my head.

When I first bought my townhouse I converted my garage into an exercise room. My treadmill was used for a clothes hanger. Being in MAP, I sponsor four girls who each talk for fifteen minutes every morning. That was an hour every day of sitting in a chair, on the couch, or in bed talking and listening. God reminded me that I could be on my treadmill during those calls. What a great idea, I didn't have to find extra time; I just needed to put my sneakers on while taking my calls. It sounded like a great idea, but I wasn't sure how I was going to feel about it at 5:55 a.m.

Just as He promised, when the alarm went off the next morning, I immediately woke up. I jumped out of bed, put my sneakers on and I was downstairs on the treadmill one minute before my phone rang. That was God doing for me what I could not do for myself. He also reminded me that a headset I purchased years before would be perfect while taking these calls. That was many moons ago and I still stick to that routine five times a week. God is still my personal trainer. How awesome is that?

## The Celtics Championship

I arrived at work my usual time of 8:03. The Boston Celtics had won the National Basketball Association Championship the night before. As the office manager I was responsible for all the festivities for the employees. Several people asked me if we were going to do anything special to celebrate the championship. We were always looking for reasons to party. After completing my opening routine I hopped back in my car and went to the market. I wanted something green for the Celtic colors but didn't have much luck. The usual donut holes, fresh fruit, and mini-cupcakes were in my basket. On my way out I saw shamrock colored gumdrops...perfect. When the cashier finished ringing up the goodies she told me the total was $33.33. It made me smile. What

89

are the chances of having it total thirty-three dollars and thirty-three cents? God was smiling down and giving me one of His *God-winks*. I lovingly looked up in acknowledgment.

After the snacks were spread out in the lunchroom, I made a copy of my receipt for reimbursement. Can you imagine my delight as I noticed the time these items were bought was 8:33:33? I never noticed the time on any of my other receipts. This day the 33s were all over the paper. This was a total *God-HUG*, let alone a *God-wink*. I loved that receipt so much that it is now laminated. What are the chances? Only God could make this happen: $33.33 was purchased at 8:33:33.

**The Secret**

There was much buzz about the book and movie, *The Secret,* but I didn't have a spare minute for any of it. I had just started getting involved in a new project and I was spending every waking hour doing research.

My last five cars were Saturns. Their outside surface wouldn't easily get those annoying dings from shopping carts, car doors opening into them, or even from road rocks. It was recently announced that the Saturn car would no longer be made with ding-proof polymer. I started to rethink my choice. It was February, 2007, in New Hampshire, and it was one of the mildest winters on record. Ford had just released a retro Mustang convertible and they seemed to be everywhere.

While having coffee with my friends, Jeanne and Jan, they couldn't stop talking about *The Secret.* They told me about the Law of Attraction. I chimed into the conversation saying, "I'm seeing Mustang convertibles everywhere." They implored me to get *The Secret.* I walked over to Target while they were still having their coffee and bought the CDs. That was Saturday morning.

I loved almost everything about the CD's. I just substituted The Universe and replaced it with God. One of the things *The Secret* talks about is if you are attracted to a car, house, boat, whatever, you need to know how much it cost. If you have one to sell, figure out how much it's worth. I spent the weekend investigating Mustang convertibles. On Tuesday it was time to regroup and do my taxes. Before starting the tax forms I proclaimed, "I would like to get at least $1000 back from my tax return." TurboTax lets you see exactly how much the refund is. There is a little calculator at the top right-hand corner of the page. The refund posted $400 but I didn't accept it. I went back over my calculations. I changed one thing and it looked like a Vegas jackpot. The little meter on the top was spinning around and it stopped at $1,033. I was jumping for joy, and the $33 did not escape me.

The next day a car dealer called to see if I was still interested in the Mustang convertible. "What Mustang convertible?" I asked. Evidently I had filled out a form on the Internet. After talking to him for thirty minutes he told me how much he would give me for my Saturn. We agreed to meet the following evening. I had been envisioning a white car with a black convertible top but it ended up being white with a tan top. I expressed my disappointment at the tan convertible. He quickly said, "I don't know why you don't like the tan, it matches your hair." To which I replied, "Do I look like the type of gal who wants to blend in with her car?" He immediately went to his supervisor. He came back with an announcement that he could take $2,200 off the list price. I started to like that color a little bit better.

After haggling a few times on price I bought the car. The next day he delivered my gorgeous white Mustang with the tan convertible top. He took away my Saturn. It had been less than one week since I bought *The Secret* and two things had happened to me. I just laughed. It wasn't really a secret, it's just asking God and trusting, believing and receiving.

*"Ask and you will receive, and your joy will be complete."*
~ John 16:24

## The Golf Trophy

Golf is one of my favorite sports and I was thrilled to join a local co-ed golf league. There were fifty men, ten women, and we had ten teams of six golfers. Since we used handicaps, we were all evenly paired. The rules were if the opponent showed up whoever won the match would score the points. If the rival failed to attend, whoever showed up would automatically win. I quickly rose up in the ranks because of my perfect attendance, rain or shine. Several of my opponents did not. At the end of the season my name appeared in the number two spot for individual rankings. It wasn't that I was good, I just showed up more than most. Isn't that what life is all about? More than 50% of success is just showing up.

At our year-end banquet, the top three teams were recognized for their achievements. My group came in fourth. The winners were presented with fabulous trophies but it was the lady's award that I envied. It was an adorable plate with a little girl golfer, a gold-trimmed skirt, and a gold golf club. I wanted one. At that moment I swore that my team would win the next year and I would do whatever it took for us to get a trophy. At the end of the evening the organizer said, "We have a special presentation. It's the MVP Award, Most Valuable Player. We normally don't do this, but this gal has been a fabulous addition to our league. She showed up every week. She encouraged her teammates, she scheduled practices, and she was our league cheerleader. So the MVP award goes to Dyan Parker." With the league cheering he presented me with my very own trophy of the little girl with her gold-trimmed skirt and golf club. It was one of my most crowning moments. That trophy has a prominent place in my living room so it will never go undetected. It's a constant reminder to show up, do my best, and encourage others.

## CEU-333

Years ago, when I moved to New Hampshire from Massachusetts, I needed to get a new state license plate. At City Hall I asked the person behind the counter if I had to take the next plate in the pile or could a special plate be requested. 33 was my "God number" and I would love to have 33 somewhere in my license plate. She gave me a condescending look as she walked into the back room. I waited over twenty minutes, thinking that perhaps she forgot about me and went to lunch. When she finally came back she had a set of license plates under her armpit. She produced them saying, "This was the best I could do." The plates read CEU-333. I was thrilled. She had just earned a feather in her angel wings and I was jumping for joy.

Many people would ask me if the CEU on my plate meant Continuing Education Units or Certified Employment Union. I would simply say, "333 is a God number but the CEU doesn't mean anything." That all changed years later when I parked in front of a Brazilian Church in my adorable Mustang convertible. It was a glorious day so the top was down. A young man was getting out of church with his family and made a comment about my great car. As he backed up he added, "I love your license plate, too, where did you get that?" I recited the City Hall story and ended, as always, with "333 is a God number but the CEU doesn't mean anything." He then replied, "Oh, yes it does." "Really? What?" I asked. He claimed, "CEU means Heaven in Portuguese." I could hardly believe my ears. CEU could have meant dog or turnip but it meant Heaven? I couldn't wait to get home to check the Portuguese dictionary on line. Sure enough, CEU in the Portuguese dictionary means Heaven or sky. For fifteen years I had been driving around with that license plate. All the time it said *Heaven – Jesus*...now that really got my attention. I just laughed, looked up to Heaven and said, "You are amazing."

## Kicked to the Curb

ISO was sold after I had been working there for three years. They terminated most of the top executives and several of the consultants. The office manager would be the last one standing, or so I thought. You can imagine my shock when I got kicked to the curb a few weeks later. They did it gently, however, and said that they loved me but didn't need me full-time. They only wanted me half the time, twenty hours. They also wouldn't be paying me what I averaged hourly, since I was on salary. They would be paying half of that. Doing some quick math, I figured that it would be 25% of my normal take home; less than unemployment. They also told me they would pay me twenty-six days of vacation, which surprised me. Since this was in February, I hadn't accrued twenty-six days yet. That's how many would be in my account by the end of the year. I made a mental note of thinking how generous they were. That was premature on my part. The second round of paperwork stated they were paying me for twenty-six *hours*, not twenty-six days. Thankfully, my signature was already on the first agreement. They were obligated to pay me the days, instead of hours. One little word, days instead of hours, was over a $6,000 error in my favor. Isn't God great?

# CHAPTER 11 ~ ATTITUDE OF GRATITUDE

*"Give thanks to the Lord, for He is good. His love endures forever."* ~ Psalm 136:1

## Get a Vanity Plate

The day after I got kicked to the curb, my friend Peter S commented, "You just got laid off? I have something you might be interested in." He continued to tell me about an interesting company. I was on my way to Aspen again, my winter ritual, and didn't have much time to chat. Peter did say, "Somebody big is buying into us. They can't tell us who it is yet but they say it's bigger than Oprah." My response was, "Who's bigger than Oprah?" A few weeks later, while skiing on the slopes of Snowmass, my cell phone rang. Peter was on the other end and all he said was, "Donald Trump. Donald Trump. Donald Trump is the one who's buying into us." I screamed, "I'm in," and couldn't wait to get home to New Hampshire.

My business excelled over the next five months. One night I was awakened at 2 a.m. from a deep sleep with the strong command to *"Get a vanity plate."* It was an odd directive but I got out of bed and turned on my computer. I didn't even know where to begin. I Googled "Vanity Plates New Hampshire" and up popped a page with a little blank license plate. It asked what I wanted to put on that plate. Still half asleep, I semi-replied to my computer "I'm not quite sure, it wasn't my idea. I'm assuming Trump." TRUMP was already taken. It suggested adding symbols before or after so I tried +TRUMP+. It was available. This was Sunday night. My license needed renewing sometime in August. I decided to go to the registry the following morning.

Little did I know that Monday was August third. It was the first available day that I could have changed my plate. In New Hampshire you can only change your license plate during the month of your birthday. God was so good to not give me that inspiration about getting a Trump plate in March, April, May, June, or July. He gave me the inspiration the exact moment that I could request that vanity plate. Because we were highly regulated we weren't supposed to even use the Trump name in anything. A few people told me I would get in trouble for having the signature title on my car. I just laughed and said to myself, "It wasn't my idea. God's the one who told me to get this. I'm sure He knows the rules."

**More Dragonflies**

The official launch of my new business with The Trump Network was in Miami. I was disappointed in myself for not bringing fifteen people with me. I would have been able to get a picture with Donald Trump for my accomplishments. At the airport I picked up

Trump's latest book *Think like a Champion*. Scott, a founder of TTN, saw me reading it. He suggested that I take the book to the Red Carpet event. Perhaps Mr. Trump would sign it. What a great idea; it would have never crossed my mind.

The gala evening finally arrived and there were five-thousand people inside the hotel. Somebody said that it was not a red carpet but a purple carpet because purple was the color of our logo. I ventured outside in the glorious Miami weather to check out that carpet. My book, pen and video camera were ready for my big moment, should it present itself.

There were already several hundred people outside. I started schmoozing with the security guys. Many people were getting agitated, complaining that they had already been waiting over forty-five minutes for Mr. Trump. I was shocked that they couldn't appreciate the fabulous weather. It was a spectacular evening and I said out loud, to no one in particular, "What a gorgeous night. Are we blessed or what? Thank God it's not raining and it's such a stunning evening. We should be thrilled to be able to be outside in such lovely weather. Thank You, God." Those words were no sooner out of my mouth when a swarm of huge dragonflies danced above our heads. It made me laugh as I felt God saying, *"Thank you for the praise, thank you for your happy heart."*

Security then received word that the motorcade was on its way. We all needed to move back on to the sidewalk. I ended up in the front row, about ten people to the left of the carpet. My friend Emily had offered to take a video of the book signing, if the opportunity arose. The three founders were getting in position on the purple carpet. I raised my book and yelled, "Scott, I have my book with me." He gave me a huge grin and two thumbs up. I was standing in the first row, with the security guards in front of me. Suddenly the entire security row, in unison, went perpendicular to me. Their bodies extended the purple carpet up to where the motorcade would be stopping. Although still in the front row, I was now totally boxed out, looking at the backs of the security guards, with no chance of Trump passing by me.

Something possessed me to yell, "Scott, where do you want me?" It was a joke since I had been kidding for most of my time outside. Scott looked at me, shook his head in sheer amusement. He laughed and motioned for me to join him on the purple carpet. Scooting through the security guards I said, "He told me to come, he told me to come." They all laughed and replied, "We know. We heard him." Emily, my camera gal, followed closely behind. Scott said, "Dyan, we need to talk with him first. After that he's yours." I couldn't believe my ears. It all happened so fast.

The shiny, black convoy arrived and Mr. Trump stepped out of the limo. The crowd came unglued. The founders shook his hand as thousands of flashbulbs glittered the sky. The theme from *The Apprentice* permeated the air. The four of them were only inches away from me. Holding my book in one hand, my pen in the other, and wearing my biggest smile, I was jumping out of my skin. Mr. Trump turned to me, signed my book, as Emily directed, "Move in, Dy, move in." I leaned into Mr. Trump as if we were dating and gave a brilliant smile to my photographer. She cracked up and laughed hysterically. Within the priceless video was a clip that was voted the Best Picture of the Launch. Forget about being in one of the posed group pictures. I had my thirty-three seconds in the limelight and was absolutely ecstatic. God was certainly looking out for me that evening.

## The Blonde in the Convertible

After the big launch of TTN several of us stayed in Miami for a few more days. One night six of us walked over to a restaurant a few blocks away from our hotel. The place was packed. Being sober makes me more aware of people who drink alcohol. My protective instincts tend to come out. We separated into pairs to be safe; at least we had each other. My friend Pauline and I wanted to go to South Beach. We said our goodbyes and planned to meet everyone back at the hotel a few hours later.

South Beach is always fun with so much happening. There are many exciting things to see, and even more to do. It was so lovely outside we didn't want the evening to end. We stayed out quite late and reluctantly hopped in a taxi to go back to our hotel. We were driving over one of the many bridges. I noticed we were approaching a gorgeous black Mercedes convertible with the top down. A man was driving. Another male crouched in the back. In the passenger seat sat a woman with beautiful blonde hair blowing in the wind. Other than making a mental note of what a spectacular evening it was for a convertible, I didn't think anything about it, until our taxi passed them. Casually glancing their way for just a moment, I was shocked to see that the blonde was my friend Deb. She had been well on her way to being drunk when we left her at the club hours before. I could only imagine her current state of mind.

Deb liked to drink and I was sure she was intoxicated. As I put down the window and yelled "Deb" the driver didn't look at me with surprise, but with fear. He just got caught. In that instant I realized that my friend was in trouble. This all happened in an instant. It was only by the Grace of God that we saw her. We also saw who she was with. I had never seen a guilty man, but saw one that night. The road was soon dividing, our hotel was to the left, the lane we were in. The convertible was in the far right, with no intention of going back to the hotel. I got a real sick feeling in the pit of my stomach as the convertible drove off in the opposite direction. It was soon out of sight.

When the taxi dropped us off at the hotel, which was only a few blocks away, I waited outside. I was not sure of what to do about Deb. Within minutes the black Mercedes convertible drove up and quickly dropped her off. Deb was too polluted to even know that she was in danger. I made eye contact with the driver. He knew that I knew. He had no intention of returning her until we caught him on that bridge. My only words to him were, "Thank you for bringing her back." He knew what I meant.

I know without a shadow of a doubt we would have never seen Deb again. God was the only one that could have allowed that interception. There were too many chains of events and perfect timings that had to happen. Both cars were in the exact spot at that exact time. I'm so grateful that God allowed me to save her life. As I recall this story it just turned 33° outside.

## Breakfast with Trump

I love contests. The first contest with The Trump Network was "Win a Breakfast with Donald Trump." The rules were that we had to enroll at least one new person every month for five months. We would then be invited to The Trump Tower to have breakfast with The Donald, as he so fondly loved to be called. My mind was focused and determined; I wanted to have breakfast with Mr. Trump. Although a few people said they would join that first month, for one reason or another it didn't happen. There were only six more hours left till the end of the first month. I needed to get my first recruit or I would not be eligible to continue the contest. There were absolutely no prospects in sight. At my MAP meeting at 5:30 in the evening I heard something that made me think. Margaret said, "I was having an issue so I asked God for help." I had forgotten to ask God for help. Sitting in the meeting, I silently said to Him, "God, only You know how hard I have been working. Please help me enroll someone before the end of the evening, if You think I deserve it. If You don't, I will accept that. Thank You in advance."

Fifteen minutes after leaving that meeting my phone rang. It was my friend Beth. She said, "I am going to get slammed on my taxes this year." My quick reply was, "You need a home-based business." She said, "Sign me up." I was amazed, elated and grateful. I was also happy that I heard the reminder to ask God for help. I totally forgot that the King of the Universe was on my side. I could ask Him for help anytime. He always helps when I remember to ask Him. That's a prize in itself. What can be better than that?

## Do You Know Jesus?

The first time I met Sharon was at the fabric store. She had a long, blonde, big mane; she was adorable. Sharon mentioned that her husband Andy refurbished furniture. I needed my dining room table repaired so we exchanged numbers. He came over to check it out and he agreed to restore my table. Andy was just as handsome as Sharon was pretty.

As he was strapping my table in the back of his pickup, he looked at me and asked, "Do you know Jesus?" I smiled and said, "Absolutely. I not only know Jesus, He has spoken to me several times." For the next three hours, standing out in my driveway, we exchanged God stories; it was amazing. Sharon and Andy are two of my favorite people. My table came out lovely and I'm so glad that God put them in my life.

## In the Rearview Mirror

My friend Betty was getting her MBA in Divinity and she hired me to type her papers. This was right up my alley. I loved listening to Betty rattle off her spiritual interpretation of the Bible. One of the courses was about corruption and how it all pointed back to Satan. This tied in with my personal philosophy and my belief in God. Betty and I would get into deep discussions on how cunning, baffling and powerful the devil could be. She had just finished writing an excellent exposé about the evil in the world.

On my drive home that afternoon while stopped at a red light, I casually glanced in my rearview mirror and saw Satan in the car behind me. My heart almost jumped out of my chest in fright. Can you imagine my terror? It was the devil sitting at the steering wheel and in his silhouette I could see horns. It wouldn't have hit me so hard but we had just been discussing Satan. It was in the front of my brain and there he was, in the car behind me. It freaked me out. I was petrified to look again in my rearview mirror but I couldn't help myself.

This time I could more clearly see a man with sunglasses on the top of his head. Although that's what it ended up being, I know that the evil one was smirking. He was telling me, "I'm around." I just said, "Thank You, Jesus, and protect me, Jesus. Satan, get behind me in the name of Jesus." He literally *was* behind me. Let me tell you that was one freaky moment.

**The Passion**

My friend Dave and I would meet at Church most Saturday evenings. One night the church parking lot was empty except for other uninformed parishioners. We soon realized that it was Holy Saturday, the day between Good Friday and Easter. There would not be a 5:00 Service, only the Easter Vigil, hours later. We decided to go out for dinner instead.

On my way back to my house I was disappointed not to attend Mass on this most holy of nights. It was still early and I didn't have anything on my schedule when the thought crossed my mind to watch a DVD. I couldn't remember the last time that I watched a movie. Looking through my bookshelf, *The Passion* appeared in my movie collection. I definitely didn't buy it. I never saw it in my bookcase before that night nor do I remember anyone giving it to me. I was thrilled – what a wonderful surprise.

Watching the last hours of Christ was heart wrenching. To say that *The Passion* was emotional is an understatement. Evidently, it was something that I needed to watch. God's timing is always perfect. He waited for the best time to present that movie and He lined it all up to perfection. I love the way He works in my life.

# CHAPTER 12 ~ BLESSED & HIGHLY FAVORED

*"Dear friend, I pray that you may enjoy good health and that all may go well with you."* ~ 3 John 1:2

## My Dad

When my dad took sick, and did not recover from a simple surgery, he went to rehab at a nursing home. After weeks of exercises he did not improve and needed to stay in that facility. We were devastated. He would not be able to go home because he "forgot" how to walk. I was working for myself at the time and would make the hour-long drive every Monday, Wednesday and weekends to have lunch with him. My mother would be able to continue to take her dance lessons, which she loved and had been doing for years. She would visit him during the evenings.

We soon worked out a schedule and that became our norm. My dad had always been a card shark; it's in his blood. Since he loved cards, I bought poker chips and a few decks of cards. We played often. On the nice days I would take my dad outside or go for a ride in my convertible, which he thoroughly enjoyed. Ice cream at Bliss Brothers was always the destination. I would park under a tree and we would sit in the car and enjoy conversation and sugar-free ice cream. Although my dad is a big man, I had been able to get him in and out of my low riding car with minimal effort.

This routine continued until my mom was unable to drive at night. She would only be able to visit him during the day. My scheduled also changed at the same time and I would not be able to see my dad on weekdays. Isn't God amazing? My dad loved the new routine, too, because my mom would take naps with him. Isn't that just adorable?

## Parades

My dad was a Navy Veteran. For six years we had been in every Veterans Day, 4th of July, and the Memorial Day Parade. If there was a parade we were in it. It all started the first year that I was going just to watch him in a parade. My mother and I were driving towards the location where we would be standing. I asked her about the float that my dad would be on. She replied, "Oh, the float is broken, they're going to be walking" "Walking?" I asked incredulously, "How far do they have to walk?" My mother thought it was three or four miles. My astonished reply was, "Three or four miles? He's eighty-two years old. He can't walk three or four miles."

At that point it dawned on me that we were in my new convertible. We could put the top down and he could sit in the back. We turned around and headed towards the parade lineup. I found my father and told him of our plan. He and his friend Mickey got in the back seat and they were able to ride while my mother and I sat up front.

We were both wearing our USA Olympic berets for the festivities so it looked like we planned to be part of the parade, too.

That became our tradition. If there was a parade I got the call from my dad, "Dy, what are you doing Memorial Day?" (Or whatever the upcoming holiday was.) My reply would always be, "I guess I'll be in a parade with you, Dad." We would buy $100 worth of candy. It was a wonderful honor and a privilege to be riding with my dad during the parades. To see the hundreds of people clapping for his service was quite emotional. The first year it was good that I was wearing sunglasses because I was crying behind my shades. I never understood the depth of his service or what it meant to my life and to every one of the bystanders. The gratitude that was expressed made me appreciate my father even more than I always had. We continued to ride in parades, even though my dad was in the nursing home. His legs did not work properly but he still knew how to toss candy.

**Naval Angel**

The last parade my dad and I were in was July 4, 2013. After the ceremony, while wheeling him back to my car, I noticed there was another Mustang parked behind me. The young Master of Ceremonies was getting into it. When he saw that the white Mustang convertible was mine we started talking Mustangs. My mother, father and I then went to have lunch and ice cream.

Halfway through the meal my dad announced that he had to use the restroom. I was not prepared for that and panicked.

My dad has been out with me many times and he's never needed to use the restroom until then. Since the nursing home was three miles from the restaurant I didn't know what to do. My instant solution was to try to hurry and get him in the car, quickly drive him back to the nursing home, swiftly get him out of the car, briskly wheel him into the elevator, and frantically get somebody to assist him before he had an accident. I started to come unglued. I told my mother to stay where she was and that I'd be back. I whisked my dad out of the restaurant as fast as I could. Halfway through the parking lot I heard someone yell, "Are you following me?" It was the Master of Ceremonies just getting out of his Mustang. I turned my father back in the direction of the restaurant and yelled to the Officer, "I need your help."

We were at the men's room in the blink of an eye with the young Navy man running behind me. I said, "My dad needs to use the bathroom, would you please help him?" He gave me a resounding, "Absolutely, it would be my pleasure." I was able to go back to my mother, take a deep breath, and explain the wonderful change of plans. My dad was grateful and happy to continue his meal. I couldn't thank that young man enough and he proudly said,

"Anything for a Veteran." Thank You, God, for sending me a Naval Angel. All dressed in white he really did look like an Angel.

## I'm Blessed and Highly Favored

Every time I called this equipment company Steve would pleasantly answer the phone. When I asked how he was, his reply was always, "I'm blessed and highly favored." That was such an interesting comment, and it always made me smile. My response was, "Me, too." After speaking with him a few times, hearing the same reply, I decided to say that when somebody asked me how I was. Because the truth is, *"I am blessed and highly favored."*

## My Amazing Parents

Two of my biggest blessings in my life have been my parents. They are amazing; not perfect, but amazing. My mother was wise beyond her years as a young mother. She did not have the best upbringing with an alcoholic dad and a loving but passive mother. My mom knew she wanted a different life for her children. My older brother was an angel. He was the blond haired, blue eyed, firstborn Prince. Fourteen months later I came into the world screaming. My black hair stuck out all over. With my violet eyes and red skin my mother thought the nurse gave her the wrong baby. I was born compulsive, wanting more, but more was never enough. I wanted more attention, more food, more love, more toys, more of anything and everything. I was really bad compared to my angelic brother. My mother knew that keeping me in the corner was no way for a toddler to be raised. She couldn't keep yelling at me because she knew it wasn't my fault: I was born with a wild personality. She's told me years later that she tried very hard not to break my spirit. She saw that I had a different temperament, special but difficult. I excelled in everything and although my brother was older I helped him with his homework. When my two sisters were born I was jealous of them because I wanted to be the only daughter. Thank God that attitude changed once I matured and now my sisters are my best friends.

My dad was wonderful also; he would do anything for his family. He liked to gamble a little too much which didn't please my mother. She had a tight budget, a household to run and four growing children. She needed every dime. You can imagine the frustration aimed at my father when he would lose any amount of money. But my dad had a big heart; he was there for us, always. If I needed a ride, help with a science project, or supper brought to me while I was teaching dance, my dad was there. He was also very handsome; many of my friends had a crush on him. God has blessed me with amazing parents and I love them dearly. I was always so proud that they were my parents.

## Yes Is in Your Future

As a Champion of Hope with Joel Osteen Ministries, I received several of his CDs. One of the latest is a series called *SUDDENLY*. It has a disc called "Yes Is in Your Future." This is one of my favorite CDs. I've listened to it more times than I can count. Since I don't have a TV, the sleep timer gets set and the CD plays. I fall asleep listening to wonderful inspirational messages.

My mother had a heart attack recently so I was at her house and was not able to listen to my nightly CDs. Since we were also not able to go to church on Sunday I checked to see if Joel was on TV. We were fortunate enough to watch his program within minutes of searching the guide.

You will never guess what show we were about to watch. "Yes Is in Your Future." It made me laugh. It was my favorite CD and I was now able to *see* Joel as he was recording it. What are the chances of me watching my favorite CD? Only God could have done it and it made me smile. The following Wednesday, while still at Mom's I saw that Joel was on again. I turned to the correct station and was blessed with one more time of seeing "Yes Is in Your Future". Isn't God amazing? I think He's trying to tell me that YES *is* in my future.

## Nantucket

Every summer my sister, Pat, and her wonderful husband, Peter, rent a large house on Nantucket. They invite our entire family of twenty-five people and three dogs. We spend the week with them, either right on the beach or in the center of town. This is real evidence that we get along and love each other. We are all under one roof and we have happy pictures to prove it.

Early one evening we were corralling the gang for our annual photo shoot at Dionis Beach. Everyone squeezed into four cars and a taxi. We were patiently waiting for Ralph to lock up the house. He came outside and somewhat frantically announced to everyone, "I smell something burning." His wife Ivy unbuckled her seat belt and went inside to investigate. We all waited in our cars; there was a small window of time to catch the sunset and daylight was burning. Evidently that was not the only thing on fire.

Ivy came to the screen door and yelled, "It's coming from Auntie's room." Yikes, I had just finished using my hot rollers. I assured everyone that the curlers were probably the source of the odor and went inside to check. I was wrong. Something was definitely burning in my room and it was not the smell of my rollers. We couldn't find the source. The three of us continued to sniff every inch of the room. That's when Ivy discovered a smoldering towel on a high wall sconce. This suppressed combustion had full intention of destroying the old wooden home.

The bath towel that I so innocently placed on the only 'hook' in my bedroom was the culprit. Not wanting to put a damp towel on the stunning antique furniture the light sconce was a great spot. It was the perfect option until my sister, Nancy, came in the room and flipped on the light switch. Since the towel blocked the bulb, she didn't realize a light was even turned on. An hour later it was hot enough to burn through the fabric. In another hour the house would have been fully engulfed.

God was with us that evening. Our personal safety was not in jeopardy because we would have been away at the beach taking pictures. The hundred-year-old home would have gone up within minutes due to the ancient, brittle wooden structure. We were also in the congested center of town. The proximity of the neighbors would have put many others in danger, too. I am thankful that Ralph was so conscientious. He was recently honored as one of the "36 Reasons to Love Rhode Island" because he is a super brainiac. We were all grateful that Ralph's brain and *nose* were working overtime that hot summer evening.

## The Glasses

Kathleen called in her usual panic. Everything was always a crisis for her. Her driver's license renewal was coming up. She would have to take the eye test and she lost her glasses. The SOS call was for me to find glasses for her. Since I had a week to complete this mission, I asked my mother and friends for donations to the cause.

When I picked her up at the bus station she immediately tried on the donated glasses. Only one pair out of ten might work. We drove to the Registry of Motor Vehicles and took our chances.

They called her name. Kathleen surprised me because she started complimenting the woman at the front desk who was in charge of the eye exam. Kathleen told her how young she looked and how cute she was. It was quite entertaining. I have a friend who worked there who was not always as complimentary about this gal. Regardless, the woman was quite flattered and asked her to read line one. I assumed it was the easiest option. Kathleen didn't put on the glasses when she looked at the vision test. She continued to rattle off ten or twelve letters and numbers. I listened in shock. She always needed glasses to see the screen, so I wasn't sure if she was reading them correctly. The woman behind the desk said in a cheerful voice, "Perfect." It was hard trying to cover up my amazement. Kathleen felt the same. This was the first time that she did not have a "C" on her license for corrective lenses. We both walked away in disbelief. She confided to me that for a split second she could see those letters perfectly. When she rattled off the last letter she totally lost her focus and they became blurred again. We both agreed it was nothing short of a miracle, a true *God-wink*.

Three weeks later while going down to see my family I noticed a bag on the floor in the back of my car. It was filled with the glasses. I had forgotten that they were there. That day I went to see my grandmother who at the time was almost 101 and in a lovely assisted living residence. She told me that she had broken her glasses and needed them repaired. I just happen to have the bag of glasses that I found just hours before. Lo and behold, the first pair that Gram tried on were perfect. She was so excited. My Uncle Ronnie was there and she asked him to put the TV on and said, "I love them. Now I can see the TV." When asked if she still wanted her broken glasses repaired she said no. The new glasses were so much better than her old pair. Ronnie was eyeing the bag so I suggested that he try some on. It's always smart to have a spare. Two pair were perfect for Uncle Ronnie. Kathleen did not need the glasses but they were ideal for Gram and my uncle. Had I not seen that bag in the back seat I would have never even remembered that I had a winning assortment. Again, isn't God good?

# CHAPTER 13 ~ A HAPPY HEART

*"And if you faithfully obey the Voice of the Lord your God,*
*being careful to do all His commandments that I command*
*you today, the Lord your God will set you high above all*
*the nations of the earth."* ~ Deuteronomy 28:1

## SISEL

SISEL (sizzle) International is an amazing company. The Trump
Network was having financial difficulties so the founder of SISEL
was going to buy them. Tom M wanted to help get them back on
their feet. TTN had too much obvious debt, let alone what would
surface once the company was acquired. SISEL decided it was not
in their best interest to make the purchase. That's when most of us
left TTN and joined Sisel. TTN quickly went bankrupt.

It soon was clear that TTN was just the dress rehearsal, and SISEL
was the real deal. We went from the Flintstones to the Jetsons and
from Kindergarten to Grad School. It felt like I had been with a
lousy boyfriend and was now in an amazing relationship.
Everything about SISEL sizzled.

## Check Out Other Airlines

My team was #1 in the country and we were invited to the SISEL
Home Office. We were thrilled. We would have training in Tom's
home, the largest house west of the Mississippi, staying at his

multimillion dollar log cabin in the mountains of Utah. I couldn't afford to go but I definitely couldn't afford *not* to go.

All expenses were paid except the airfare. The flights to Utah were somewhat expensive. When we won this event, my brain went into a mini tailspin. I wasn't sure how it would unfold, if I would get new customers or distributors but I just HAD-TO-GO. My friend Laura had already booked her ticket on Southwest and it was $400…$400 more than I had available.

That night, while driving, God whispered in my ear, *"Check out other airlines."* I had a few airline numbers in my phone address book. All I had to do was touch the word United Airlines and my phone started to dial. The automated system stated, "We looked up your account. Is this your first name, spelled DYAN? Yes or No." When I replied, "Yes," it continued. "Are you calling to make a new reservation, to change an existing reservation, Mileage Plus, or more options?" I didn't think there were any miles left in my account but said to the automated agent, "Mileage Plus." I heard the little calculations were going on in the background. It came back and said, "You have 44,000 miles." WOW, cool. They were forgotten miles. A Super Saver award would only be 25,000 miles. It started to excite me. Speaking to an agent she confirmed that United flew from Boston to Salt Lake City. They had a Super Saver available. Once home, a flight was booked within hours of

Laura's flight and it cost a total of ten dollars. My flight to Utah was only ten dollars!

The evening before I woke up in the middle of the night as I often do and looked at the clock; it was 3:33. There was such a sense of peace that everything will be all right, and not to worry about anything. All is well. Sometimes panic hits me about the bills getting paid. The money certainly goes out much faster than it comes in. When God tells me not to worry about anything I need not worry about anything. Everything will be all right.

I was thrilled that He whispered, *"Check out other airlines."* I would have never ever remembered there were award miles sitting in my account. It was by calling the automated system that really brought this all together. I called seconds after God gave me the inspiration to check out other airlines. Thank You, God, for whispering in my ear. You are amazing.

Before we left for the trip, I was on Facebook and found a lucky person who lived near the home office. Lisa P joined us for dinner our first night in Utah, came on the tour the next day, and was invited to Tom's house. She joined the business. How fortunate for Lisa that she was able to receive the VIP treatment on day one. I was so happy and proud that she is on my team.

## I Wanted the Bouquet

When my girlfriend LA got married I knew that her husband's brother Bill would also be at the wedding. He was recently single. LA had mentioned that we might make a good match because we had lots in common. Since there was no one that I wanted to spend the entire day with, I didn't bring a date. Most of the wedding guests were couples but there were four single girls at my table. When it was time for the garter toss Bill caught it. Then LA threw the bouquet. I had a thought earlier that day. "Wouldn't that be interesting if Bill grabbed the garter and I caught the bouquet?" That was all, just a quick passing thought, but that was something that had crossed my mind. When LA tossed the bouquet it went right into Sue's arms. "Oh well, no big deal," is what I thought and walked off the dance floor.

When the DJ called Sue and Bill up to the floor it was discovered they were cousins. The DJ told LA that Bill needed to have somebody else to put the garter on. LA didn't hesitate as she yelled out, "Dyan Parker." I just laughed and thought, "Why not. This is how I had envisioned it." Off to the dance floor I went. You know how it goes. They get the lone chair for the girl to sit on, the man starts to put the garter up her leg. Then the DJ says, "Oops, wrong leg." He takes it down, only to put it on the other leg...it was cute and I was glad my legs were shaved.

122

It was a sweet little *God-wink* for my desire to come true even if it was indirectly. Oh, by the way, I won the centerpiece, so I did go home with flowers.

## The Gal at the Wedding

Paul, an old neighbor, brought me to another wedding. His lovely wife Connie passed away years ago and he didn't want to go alone. He's a wonderful man and he can always count on me if he needs a date. It's fun to meet new people. I always ask God to introduce me to new friends and interesting prospects. God did not disappoint me when we were getting ready to leave. A beautiful gal, Lisa M, had come to our table to talk with her cousins about body wraps. She was not only selling them but had experienced a six-inch-loss after using them a few times. That did not impress me at all. I had just lost seventeen inches in three months with SISEL products and that made more sense to me than wraps. We exchanged numbers, swapped stories a week later and she loved what she saw in SISEL. We need to learn how to eat better, not get shrink-wrapped. The following week Lisa M. became one of my business partners.

## Letter of Recommendation

There was an opening for mental health assistant at a local facility. I was definitely overqualified for this job but working only three days a week was appealing. I met all the requirements except one. Must have experience working in the mental health field. Kiddingly I said out loud, "I've been in the dating game for several years now, I know all about mental health." That was not included on my resume since they probably wouldn't appreciate my humor.

Several mental health facilities include addictions: alcohol, food, gambling, almost anything. Then I remembered working at an alcohol and drug rehab hospital years ago while living in Georgia. At the time, we received hard copies of letters of recommendation. It had been many years since working there, but there was a possibility that a letter from them was in my file. On the side of my desk was a sheet protector and sure enough their letter was right on top. You can imagine my delight when I took out that paper and read a wonderful recommendation. Although it was years ago, qualities, values, and skills don't change. I possessed them then and still have them today. It also included my title of Mental Health Assistant. I scanned the recommendation, included it with my cover letter along with my resume. I didn't get that job, but I would have never remembered having worked in the mental health field or that there was a letter of recommendation or being able to find it. What are the chances of that? Again, only God could have pulled off that trick. It makes me smile every time He does something like this because it just confirms that He's got my back. Thanks, God.

## I Didn't Know You Were Looking for a Job

My friend Ann heard me tell the story about finding the old letter of recommendation. She didn't know I was looking for a job. She then told me of a company that needed an office assistant. I applied for it, only to find that another friend works there. Ron put in a good word and they hired me. This is the perfect position for me. Everyone is helpful and it's within three miles of my home.

# CHAPTER 14 ~ GOD IS ALWAYS HERE

*"Sing joyfully to the Lord, you righteous; it is fitting for the upright to praise him." ~* Psalm 33:1

## B33 IOU

There was a truck parked right behind me with a license plate that said B33 IOU. It made me laugh. I felt God was saying, *"Be like me, be 33. I owe you"* or *"If you keep sharing My Word I'll owe you ~ you need me and I need you."*

## My Friend Dennis

It was early December 2011 and I had just returned from Florida. Driving up to the MAP meeting I noticed my friend Diane getting out of her car. My mind immediately went to how blessed she was. She and her wonderful husband Dennis have four grown kids and over a dozen grandchildren. Christmas was going to be just delightful this year. When I caught up with Diane and saw that she looked sad, I assumed she must be eating cookies. We are always bummed out when we eat junk. When I asked how she was doing she replied with a flat, "Okay." I challenged her and said, "Really?" She looked straight at me and said, "Dennis got killed last week." I felt as if I got kicked in the stomach, I couldn't breathe and started to sob. I had no idea. Diane was gracious as she put her arms around me and said, "I'm so sorry you had to hear about it this way." *She* started to console *me*. I could not believe it. The news was so tragic I could not control my emotions. I went from a feeling of elation for a happily married couple to an uncontrollable sadness for my widowed friend. During the meeting every time the thought of Dennis crossed my mind I would start to sob again. Diane sat next to me and tried to comfort me. She was such a pillar of strength. My heart broke for Diane, her children, and her grandchildren. Her family would never be the same without Dennis. He was one of the most amazing men I've ever met. To think that he was gone was just impossible to grasp.

The morning of his accident Dennis mentioned he needed to replace his bald tires. There was a horrific rainstorm that day. He hydroplaned on the highway, hit a tree and was killed.

A few days after the accident Diane received a call from a stranger. She asked if Di was the lady who just lost her husband. She sadly replied, "Yes." The woman continued, "Can I tell you something about your husband?" Diane hesitantly said, "Yes." The stranger continued to say that she was on the highway the day of the accident. Although she didn't see the crash she was in the backed up traffic. Her five-year-old daughter asked why they were not moving. The mother said, "There must be construction up ahead." Two minutes later the little girl said, "No, Mommy, a man just died." The mother looked at her daughter and asked why she said such a thing. The little girl sweetly replied, "Because I just saw Jesus carrying a man up to Heaven."

It was such a comfort for Diane to hear that story. As unbelievable as it sounds I know that the little girl saw Dennis being carried by Jesus. If this were ever going to happen to anyone it would happen to Dennis. That same week one of Diane's friends called her and said, "I know you're going to think this is crazy. I heard Dennis while I was at church. He said, 'I'm in Heaven. It's a real.'" These two stories are why Diane was able to console me instead of vice versa. Although she misses Dennis, she definitely knows that he is in Heaven.

## Go With the Flow

It was the mad dash of Christmas shopping. My two adorable nieces, Bella and Remi wanted kneepads for rollerblading. The Toys"R"Us parking lot was packed and the lines at the registers would be overflowing. It was the last place I wanted to be the weekend before Christmas. Trying not to dampen their spirits, I agreed to go with the kids and my mother in search of their requested presents. We entered the craziness of the store. The kneepads were not there, but on the way out the girls saw a movie they wanted to buy. Yikes, it would take hours to get through the line just to pay for one item. I was tempted to say, "No, let's not get it." At that moment I saw another register in the electronics department. It was just finishing up a transaction with a woman. There was no one behind her. There were over fifty people in line right next to that register, which was slowly snaking its way to the main check-out counters. I immediately went over and asked the cashier if we could buy the movie at her register. When she nodded, I called the kids over and quickly paid. Not only were we in and out of Toys"R"Us within minutes but the movie was also on sale, 33% off. I'm so glad that I followed my instinct to just go with the flow instead of insisting on my selfish agenda. God is good, the girls were so happy, and the movie was adorable.

## The Last Table

The girls were starving after we finished our quick trip to Toys"R"Us. Again, expecting more crowds, I silently groaned at the thought of the long wait. While we were standing in line to order, Bella and Remi scoped out the busy restaurant. They found the only available table. Our food was quickly ordered, delivered, and we were eating and chatting before we knew it. We were so happy to be together. Soon after we sat down hordes of people arrived to eat. Only God could have put us ahead of the crowd; His timing is always perfect.

That same weekend, my mother and I had Bella and Remi a little longer than usual. We attended Church on Sunday then went to see my dad in the nursing home. We all played poker and then we headed to lunch. Since my dad had been in the nursing home, my mom had not been going out to eat too often. She had tons of unused restaurant gift certificates. The girls wanted to go to CB's, which was on the property of the outlet stores. My first thought was "Yikes, no way, it will be packed, it will take us forever to get seated…no." I never realized how much I hate holiday crowds, especially when I'm hungry. I said to them while we were driving there, "Let's say a prayer that the restaurant isn't super busy. Pray that we don't have to wait too long." They repeated that prayer out loud. At the restaurant we found a parking spot right up front. We were delighted when we were seated immediately. As we sat down, we said in unison, "Thanks, God." The food was delicious and the company was even better…oh, it was also free. My mom was able to use a certificate for the bill and the tip. What a great way to end a delightful weekend with my loved ones.

## CHAPTER 15 ~ FINISH THIS BOOK

*"The Lord declares, 'Now, go, write it before them in a tablet and note it in a book that it may be for the time to come forever and ever.' "* ~ Isaiah 30:8

### Successful Authors Group

I was well on my way to writing this book when the inspiration came to check out authors or writers on Facebook. There was a page called "Successful Authors Group" which I immediately joined. Every other day I would read their latest hints, tips, concerns, and successes. It was comforting to know there were others who were writing also. Sometime in November there was a post about a writing contest sponsored by West Bow Press. God is so good; that was just the post I needed to see.

Here were the guidelines: The Author has to be unpublished: I am. The book had to be finished and submitted by January 31: I love deadlines. The minimum amount of words needs to be ten thousand: I had over thirty-thousand. Last but not least, the subject needs to be about God. How many people are writing a book about God? Mine is not only about God, it is about hearing God, about God speaking to me.

I was very excited because I love contests and usually win them. When people ask, "How will you publish your book?" my reply is always, "I haven't a clue. It wasn't my idea to write this book, it was God's." Winning the contest would certainly be the answer to that question. The fact that Women of Faith sponsored it was a huge bonus. Several of my friends had just come back from attending the WOF Conference. They said it was fabulous and every one of the speakers had written a book.

Public speaking of any kind is my dream job. Being an inspirational-motivational speaker is what I have been groomed for. Starting at an early age I loved being in front of people, acting, dancing or speaking. Anything but singing. While most people would rather be shot out of a cannon than be on stage, that's where I shine. I am not sure how this will all come together. All I know is this contest was a GIANT *God-wink*, giving me a deadline, focus, and guidelines. I have hopes of bringing even more people to know God, to know that He is real. I can do this through my story and perhaps even through inspirational speaking.

**The Perfect Job**

One more thought about my wonderful job. I was not busy. Normally that would be painful but it was not. A month after getting into the routine, God inspired me to send myself my updated writing. Every day I would edit it at work during the slow times, e-mail it back to myself at night, and work on it at home. Next day, rinse and repeat. The funny part of this is that God knew

He had to corral me and tie me down to a chair in an office. Left to my own devices I would rather be playing, skiing, going out to lunch, or folding laundry. Anything other than writing. Oh, did I mention that the extra money is also helping with my finances?

## Walk Like An Egyptian

I finally finished my book and eagerly entered the contest. The disappointment of not winning the grand prize made me put it aside for a while. Although the book was technically finished, it was a rough first draft. I knew there was much more work to do in order for it to get published. The contest was a good first goal. I took the next few months off, still thinking about the book but not picking it up often. It was always on my mind!

I had printed two copies, one for my mom and the other for me to edit in a hard copy. Once my mother finished it and passed it off to a few friends, she gave it back to me. It was as if my book had legs; I started seeing it everywhere. Since there were two copies, and I knew I needed to finish it, they were always out somewhere. They were a constant reminder that my work was not completed.

I occasionally picked it up. I always exclaimed, "I have to finish editing my book," but I did more talking than I did tweaking. It wasn't until we started doing a ninety-day-goal-exercise at work that I actually put it on my "to do" list. I had an actual plan to get it finished and start searching for an agent.

I went to a business networking event. I had the uncanny opportunity to meet a gal who does book editing and also helps people write letters to agents. Perfect! She must have been the real reason for my being at that event. She had commented that she had helped another woman write an agent letter. There were five agents fighting for the opportunity to promote her book about penguins. "I think God is more important than penguins," was my comment to myself. She gave me her card with the promise that we would stay in touch.

At the end of the evening there were several door prizes. Most were for dinners at local restaurants, free haircuts and complimentary exercise classes. Nothing of interest to me. When they announced a one-hour-free-consultation with the book editor I got excited. I wanted to win. The first two names drawn were not mine but lucky for me they had already left the event. "Walk Like an Egyptian" was playing in the background. The DJ said, "The first person to walk like an Egyptian can have this gift certificate." I was up in a flash. I had my arms flailing, looking more like Jackie Gleason than an Egyptian, but I didn't care. The gift certificate for the hour consultation was mine.

Later that night I read about this consultant. I realized how she fit perfectly into my new goal of finding an agent within the month. I saw the name of the gal who wrote the book about the penguins. Her name was not only Diane, but she spelt it like I did: D Y A N. What are the chances of that? I only laughed and said "Yes, God, I know You want me to finish this book. You are giving me all the signs and encouragement. I will be obedient and get back in the daily habit of tweaking and editing this book. Thank You for my one hour of consultation gift, I know it was from You."

I called the consultant and expressed my happiness at winning her door prize. We immediately made an appointment for two weeks from that date. I love deadlines. I work best under pressure.

## Reflecting

My hope is that this memoir will inspire the non-believer and delight the believer. Look back through your life when you thought you were lucky. May you awaken or deepen your awareness of God and give Him all the credit. Maybe even call them *God-winks*. I am certain it's all due to God's grace and favor, not coincidence or chance. I don't believe in miracles. I depend on them. I expect great things to happen to me. I pray that you develop this same confidence.

135

I'll end with the same sentiments as Professor S. Ralph, author of the story entitled *The Day We Saw the Angels*: "I have related this story with the same faithfulness and respect for truth and accuracy as I would tell it on the witness stand. But even as I record it I know how incredible it sounds."

Yes, God audibly spoke to me several times. He also speaks to my spirit by circumstances, inspirations and through other people. Let's not forget His *God-winks*. When I'm paying close attention, and looking for and listening to God, He doesn't have to speak so loud. Yes, God is real. I know He is because He spoke to me; I've heard Him. I've heard the Voice of God ~ and I'm no Angel.

*"Then I heard the Voice of the Lord saying, 'Whom shall I*
*send? And who will go for us?'*
*And I said, 'Here am I. Send me!'"* ~ Isaiah 6:8

# REFERENCES

Website: IveHeardTheVoice.com

Publisher: GenerousGiverPub.com

83605593R00095

Made in the USA
Columbia, SC
11 December 2017